CHANGE
Principles of Problem Formation and Problem Resolution

CHANGE
Principles of Problem Formation
and Problem Resolution

Paul Watzlawick
John H. Weakland
Richard Fisch
MENTAL RESEARCH INSTITUTE, PALO ALTO

Foreword by Milton H. Erickson

W · W · NORTON & COMPANY
New York · London

W. W. Norton & Company, Inc., 500 Fifth Avenue, New York, N.Y. 10110
W. W. Norton & Company Ltd., 25 New Street Square, London EC4A 3NT

Published simultaneously in Canada
by George J. McLeod Limited, Toronto

Library of Congress Cataloging in Publication Data
Watzlawick, Paul.
   Change; principles of problem formation and problem
resolution.

   Bibliography: p.
   1. Problem solving.   2.   Change (Psychology)
3.   Interpersonal relations.   I.   Weakland, John H.,
joint author.   II.   Fisch, Richard, 1926–   joint
author.   III.   Title.
BF441.W35   1974   158.2   73–17485
ISBN 0-393-01104-6

This book was designed by Nancy Dale.
Typefaces use are Video Avanta and Melior.
Manufacturing was done by Haddon Craftsmen.

Printed in the United States of America
0

To the memory of
DON D. JACKSON
(1920–1968)

CONTENTS

FOREWORD

I WOULD have preferred to say much more about this book than I do here. Unfortunately, ill health prevents me from doing that, but thereby leads me to come to the point at once.

There have been multitudes of books and theories on how to change people, but at long last, the authors in this book have looked seriously at the subject of change itself—both how change occurs spontaneously, and how change can be promoted. I have attempted to understand this in my own work, and describe it in my own writings. Psychotheraphy is sought not primarily for enlightenment about the unchangeable past but because of dissatisfaction with the present and a desire to better the future. In what direction and how much change is needed neither the patient nor the therapist can know. But a change in the current situation is required, and once established, however small, necessitates other minor changes, and a snowballing effect of these minor changes leads to other more significant changes in accord with the patient's potentials. Whether the changes are evanescent, permanent, or evolve into other changes is of vital importance in any understanding of human behavior for the self and others. I have viewed much of what I have done as expediting the currents of change already seething within the person and the family—but currents that need the "unexpected," the "illogical," and the "sudden" move to lead them into tangible fruition.

It is this phenomenon of change with which this book is concerned, the actual nature and kinds of change so long overlooked by the formulation of theories about how to change people. Watzlawick, Weakland, and Fisch have, in this extremely important book, looked at this phenomenon and put it into a conceptual framework—illuminated by examples from a variety of areas—which opens up new pathways to the further understanding of how people become enmeshed in problems with each other, and new pathways to expediting the resolution of such human impasses. The relevance of this new framework extends far beyond the sphere of "psychological" problems from which it grew. This work is fascinating. I think it is a noteworthy contribution—a damn good book—and a must for anyone seeking to understand the many aspects of group behavior.

I am pleased that my own work has contributed to the ideas represented in this book, I appreciate having had the opportunity to make this small comment on it. Perhaps, here as elsewhere, such a small gesture is all the expediting one needs do.

Phoenix, Arizona   MILTON H. ERICKSON, M.D.
November, 1973

PREFACE

Daring as it is to investigate the unknown, even more so it is to question the known.

—KASPAR

WHEN in 1334 the Duchess of Tyrol, Margareta Maultasch, encircled the castle of Hochosterwitz in the province of Carinthia, she knew only too well that the fortress, situated on an incredibly steep rock rising high above the valley floor, was impregnable to direct attack and would yield only to a long siege. In due course, the situation of the defenders became critical: they were down to their last ox and had only two bags of barley corn left. Margareta's situation was becoming equally pressing, albeit for different reasons: her troops were beginning to be unruly, there seemed to be no end to the siege in sight, and she had similarly urgent military business elsewhere. At this point the commandant of the castle decided on a desperate course of action which to his men must have seemed sheer folly: he had the last ox slaughtered, had its abdominal cavity filled with the remaining barley, and ordered the carcass thrown down the steep cliff onto a meadow in front of the enemy camp. Upon receiving this scornful message from above, the discouraged duchess abandoned the siege and moved on.

A very different situation existed in May 1940 aboard a British trawler on its way to a secret meeting with a German intelligence officer, Major Ritter, south of the Dogger Bank in the English

Channel. Aboard the ship were two "double cross" agents,[1] code-named Snow and Biscuit respectively. Snow had done excellent work for British intelligence in the past and was considered by the Germans one of their star agents in Britain. Biscuit, a man with a long criminal record, had turned into a very reliable police informer and was now to be introduced to Major Ritter as Snow's subagent, to be trained in Germany and then sent back to England. For one reason or another, British intelligence considered it advisable that neither agent should know that the other was also working for the British side, but apparently both men eventually guessed this fact. This led to a nightmarish impasse which Masterman, in his fascinating book on the British double-cross system, describes as follows:

On the way [to the rendezvous with Ritter], unfortunately, Biscuit formed the opinion from Snow's behavior and his conversation that he was acting genuinely in the interest of the Germans and would undoubtedly reveal his position as a controlled agent as soon as he met Major Ritter. Snow on the other hand appears to have been, for reasons which we cannot analyse, under the impression that Biscuit was a genuine German agent who would undoubtedly reveal his, Snow's, ambiguous position when their meeting with Ritter took place. As a result of this he did everything in his power to convince Biscuit that he was acting genuinely in the German interest, and thereby redoubled Biscuit's suspicions (75).

In this strange situation, then, both parties were trying very hard to do what under the circumstances seemed to be the best thing, but the harder they tried the more hopeless the situation became. Finally, in the interest of his own safety and to avoid what seemed to turn into a disaster for British intelligence, Biscuit

[1]This term refers either to enemy agents who are captured and "turned around" (i.e., forced to work for their captors), or to individuals who volunteer to infiltrate the enemy spy system and pose as their agents, while supplying them the right kind of wrong information, helping to uncover other enemy agents, etc.

locked Snow into his cabin and returned the trawler to Grimsby without attempting to meet Ritter. Thus, in his sincere attempt to prevent ultimate failure, he produced it.

These two examples illustrate the subject matter of this book. It deals with the age-old questions of persistence and change in human affairs. More particularly, it is concerned with how problems arise, and how they are perpetuated in some instances and resolved in others. Most of all, it examines how, paradoxically, common sense and "logical" behavior often fail, while actions as "illogical" and "unreasonable" as those taken by the defenders of Hochosterwitz succeed in producing a desired change.

On the one hand, although logic and common sense offer excellent solutions when they work, who has not had the frustrating experience of doing his very best in these terms, only to see things going from bad to worse? On the other hand, every once in a while we experience some "illogical" and surprising but welcome change in a troublesome stalemate. Indeed, the theme of the puzzling, uncommonsensical solution is an archetypical one, reflected in folklore, fairy tales, humor, and many dreams— just as there are both popular and more erudite conceptions of the perversity of other people, the world, or the devil to explain the converse situation. Yet it seems that little serious and systematic inquiry has been focused on this whole matter, which has remained as puzzling and contradictory as ever.

We ourselves came to be concerned with this problem only indirectly, largely as an unanticipated consequence of our practice and study of psychotherapy, and much of our discussion and exemplification will relate to this field with which we are most closely acquainted. Though reached via that particular route, this is primarily a book about persistence and change—and about their role in problem formation and resolution—in human affairs quite generally.

Since even our most general views relate to concrete experience, a few words about our professional background may be helpful. Like other therapists with orthodox training and many years of practical experience we found ourselves increasingly frustrated by the uncertainty of our methods, the length of treatments, and the paucity of their results. At the same time, we were intrigued by the unexpected and unexplainable success of occasional "gimmicky" interventions—probably more than anything else by the fact that they were not *supposed* to have any beneficial effect. In 1966, one of us, Richard Fisch, proposed the establishment of what for lack of a better name we came to call the Brief Therapy Center of the Mental Research Institute in Palo Alto.[2] Under his direction we began to investigate the phenomena of human change, and in doing so we soon found that this required us to take a fresh look at just about everything that we had believed, learned, and practiced.[3]

Another unifying element was the fact that from the beginning we spoke the same "language": as research associates of the Mental Research Institute we all had several years of experience in human communication research and in interactional (i.e., couple and family) psychotherapy as it had been developed by what is loosely known as the Palo Alto Group under Gregory Bateson's theoretical and Don D. Jackson's clinical leadership. We were thus accustomed to looking at process rather than content, and at the here and now rather than the past. No less important, perhaps, was the fact that we all had training and experience in

[2]The name is unsatisfactory because "brief" therapy often refers to some sort of stop-gap, superficial, or first-aid measures undertaken provisionally until "real," long-term therapy becomes possible. Barten's book *Brief Therapies* (15) probably reflects the present range of opinions on this subject quite adequately. It is composed of an excellent introduction and of articles by twenty-five authors. Of these twenty-six contributions, ten consider brief therapy methods as a form of therapy in their own right; nine see them as second-best substitutes where long-term treatment, for one reason or another, is impossible (or *not yet* possible); and seven authors describe their usefulness in what could best be summarized as "yes but no" terms.

[3]Our reason for mentioning these developments at least briefly is that otherwise the reader may be justified in wondering if we had really never heard of the unconscious, the paramount importance of the past and of insight into the past, transference, character traits and symptom substitution, and especially the dangers of manipulation.

hypnosis, which not only made us feel quite comfortable about direct interventions, but had brought us into contact with the startling and innovative techniques of Milton Erickson, to whom we all feel deeply indebted.

From the very beginning it was our assumption that by pooling our knowledge we would be able to clarify and utilize those intriguing phenomena of change mentioned earlier, and thus find new ways of intervening effectively in human problem situations. This assumption proved to be valid, but it also led to something unexpected: in designing the most appropriate form of intervention into a particular human impasse we seemed to be drawing on some underlying body of assumptions which at the time we were unable to define. This turned into somewhat of an embarrassment as more and more outsiders became familiar with and interested in our *modus operandi* through lectures, demonstrations, and training courses, and wanted to know more about our basic conceptual framework—rather than be merely impressed by some weird gimmick. In other words, they could see the effects, but wanted to know what went into their making. Only gradually were we ourselves able to conceptualize our approach, and this book is an attempt at systematizing what we found as we examined our own premises.

From past experience we fully expect to be attacked by some for the "manipulative," "insincere" nature of our approach— both practical and conceptual—to human problems. "Sincerity" has lately become a catchword, a hypocrisy in its own right, associated in a murky way with the idea that there is such a thing as a "right" view of the world—usually one's *own* view. It also seems associated with the idea that "manipulation" is not only bad, but can be avoided. Nobody, unfortunately, has ever explained how this can be done. It is difficult to imagine how *any* behavior in the presence of another person can avoid being a communication of one's own view of the nature of one's relationship with that person and how it can, therefore, fail to influence that person. The analyst who silently sits behind his reclining patient, or the "non-directive" therapist who "merely" repeats the verbal utterances of his client, exert a fantastic amount of influence *by that very behavior,* especially since it is defined as "no influence." The problem, therefore, is not how influence and manipulation can be avoided, but how they can best be comprehended and used in the interest of the patient. This is one of the subjects that will occupy us throughout this book.

We are fully aware that much of what is contained in this book has been said or done by others, although usually in different contexts and based on different premises. We hope that the reader will appreciate that not all these similarities can be pointed out, nor the differences explained. This is especially true of apparent parallelisms with behavior therapy, but the reader should bear in mind that we are not basing ourselves on assumptions of "faulty" learning and of unlearning, of conditioning and deconditioning etc.

Since this book's main aim is to present our general views and conclusions, it will not trace the long journey by which we arrived at them. Instead, as a glance at the table of contents will show, it proceeds from the abstract toward concrete, practical examples and discussion. Chapter 1, accordingly, describes two theories, useful in organizing and clarifying major aspects of our view of change at a very general level, namely the Theory of Groups and the Theory of Logical Types. Chapter 2 exemplifies the practical applicability of these two theories to our subject matter. Part II deals entirely with questions of problem formation arising out of the interdependence of persistence and change, while Part III is devoted to problem resolution.

Our thanks go first of all to the founder and first director of the Mental Research Institute, the late Dr. Don D. Jackson, whose openness to new ideas and whose help encouraged us to embark on this project. Next we want to express our appreciation to our colleague, Arthur Bodin, who was with the Brief Therapy Center for six years, as well as to Mrs. Barbara McLachlan, the untiring coordinator of the Center's activities. Our thanks also go to the other members, past and present, of the Center: Lynn Segal, Jack Simon, Tom Ferguson, Joel Latner, Paul Druckman, George Greenberg, and Frank Gerbode, and to our friend John Frykman at the Cypress Institute in Carmel.

In addition, we wish to extend our appreciation to agencies and their staff that assisted us in exploring nonclinical areas of our research: Alan Coffey and the Santa Clara County Juvenile Probation Department; Walter Morse and the Santa Clara County Adult Probation Department; Barry Bloom and Terry Burris and the San Francisco Drug Treatment Program. Other agencies were also of valuable aid, especially the Juvenile Probation Departments of San Francisco, San Mateo, Sacramento, and Monterey Counties.

We are deeply grateful to Mrs. Claire Bloom for her friendly and untiring help in the technical preparation of the manuscript.

The first year of operation of the Brief Therapy Center was made possible by a grant from the Luke B. Hancock Foundation and by matching funds received from the T. B. Walker Foundation and the Robert C. Wheeler Foundation. Their generous support is gratefully acknowledged.

PART ONE

Persistence and Change

1

THE THEORETICAL
PERSPECTIVE

Plus ça change, plus c'est la même chose.

THE French proverb according to which the more something changes the more it remains the same is more than a witticism. It is a wonderfully concise expression of the puzzling and paradoxical relationship between persistence and change. It appeals more immediately to experience than the most sophisticated theories that have been put forth by philosophers, mathematicians, and logicians, and implicitly makes a basic point often neglected: that persistence and change need to be considered together, in spite of their apparently opposite nature. This is not an abstruse idea, but a specific instance of the general principle that all perception and thought is relative, operating by comparison and contrast.

In practice, however, this comparative stance has been difficult to achieve. In the Western world the philosophers of science seem to agree that change is such a pervasive and immediate element of our experience that it could become the subject of thought only after the early Greek philosophers had been able to conceptualize the antithetical concept of invariance or persistence. Until then there was nothing that change could be conceptually contrasted with (this is a matter of conceptualizing experience, not of finding "reality"), and the situation must have been like one proposed by Whorf: that in a universe in which everything is blue, the concept of blueness cannot be developed for lack of contrasting colors.

While many theories of persistence and change have been formulated throughout the centuries of Western culture, these have mainly been theories of persistence, or theories of change, not theories of persistence and change. That is, the tendency has been either to view persistence and invariance as a "natural" or "spontaneous" state, to be taken for granted and needing no explanation, and change as the problem to be explained, or to take the inverse position. But the very fact that either position can be adopted so readily suggests that they are complementary—that what is problematic is not absolute and somehow inherent in the nature of things, but depends on the particular case and point of view involved.[1] Such a conception is consistent with our experience of human affairs and difficulties. For example, whenever we observe a person, a family, or a wider social system enmeshed in a problem in a persistent and repetitive way, despite desire and effort to alter the situation, two questions arise equally: "How does this undesirable situation persist?" and "What is required to change it?"

In the course of our work, we have made some progress not only toward answering these questions in particular cases, but in moving toward a more general view. Rather than retracing this long road, however, we feel that two abstract and general theories, drawn from the field of mathematical logic, may be utilized to help present and clarify some of the conclusions at which we have arrived. These are 1) the Theory of Groups and 2) the Theory of Logical Types.

In doing so, we are fully aware that our use of these theories is far from satisfying mathematical rigor. It should be taken as an attempt at exemplification through analogy.

---

[1]As will be observed later, problems connected with both persistence and change have been central in, and illuminated by, the development of cybernetics.

Group Theory emerged during the early part of the nineteenth century. The term *group* was introduced by the French mathematician Évariste Galois.[2] After Galois' initial formulations, several outstanding nineteenth-century mathematicians contributed to the development of Group Theory into one of the most imaginative branches of mathematics. With the revolution of classical physics after 1900 it also began to play a powerful role in quantum and relativity theory. Needless to say, the more sophisticated implications of Group Theory can be appreciated only by the mathematician or the physicist. But its basic postulates, concerned with relationships between elements and wholes, are quite simple—perhaps deceptively so. According to the theory, a *group* has the following properties:

a. It is composed of *members* which are all alike in one common characteristic, while their actual nature is otherwise irrelevant for the purposes of the theory. They can thus be numbers, objects, concepts, events, or whatever else one wants to draw together in such a group, as long as they have that common denominator and as long as the outcome of any combination of two or more members is itself a member of the group. For instance, let the members of a group be the integers 1–12, indicating the hours on the face of a clock. Then, obviously, any combination of two or more members is again a member of the group (e.g., 8:00 A.M. plus six hours takes us to 2:00 in the afternoon), and in this case *combination* refers to the process of addition or subtraction of members. Similarly, any change in the position of a die through casting will

[2]He proposed it in a brilliant paper, written in 1832 under the most unusual circumstances: Not only was Galois barely twenty years old, but he wrote the entire paper (comprising sixty pages) in one night—the night before being killed at sunrise in a duel to which he had been challenged for inane chauvinistic reasons by two "patriots." He was shot through the intestine and, with no surgeon present, simply left to die. "I have not time, I have not time," he scribbled again and again on the margin of his manuscript as he tried frantically to leave to posterity as much as he could communicate. "What he wrote in those desperate long hours before dawn will keep generations of mathematicians busy for hundreds of years," says Bell (22) about that fateful night.

give a result which is again a member of the six possible outcomes of such casting, and in this case *combination* refers to one or more rotations of the die around one or more of its three axes. We can also see that the term *combination* refers to a change from one possible internal state of the group to another.

The grouping of "things" (in the widest sense) is the most basic and necessary element of our perception and conception of reality. While it is obvious that no two things will ever be exactly alike, the ordering of the world into (complexly intersecting and overlapping) groups composed of members which all share an important element in common gives structure to what would otherwise be a phantasmagoric chaos. But as we have seen, this ordering also establishes *invariance* in the above-mentioned sense, namely that a combination of any group members is again itself a member of the group—"a thing *in* the system, not out of it," as Keyser (55) puts it. Thus this first group property may allow for myriads of changes *within* the group (in fact, there are so-called infinite groups) but also makes it impossible for any member or combination of members to place themselves *outside* the system.

b. Another property of a group is that one may combine its members in varying sequence, yet the outcome of the combination remains the same.[3] A practical example would be this: Starting from a given point on a surface and making any number of moves of any individual length and direction, one invariably and inevitably reaches the same destination, regardless of any change in the sequence of moves—provided, of course, that the number of these moves as well as their individual length and direction remain the same. The simplest case would be four moves of one unit (e.g., one yard, one mile) each in the direction of each of the four cardinal points. Regardless of the sequence (e.g., first north, then west, or whatever), under these conditions one always is back

---

[3]For instance, let a, b, and c be members of a group, and let the symbol $\underline{o}$ denote the combination rule that holds for that group. Then $(a\underline{o}b)\underline{o}c = a\underline{o}(b\underline{o}c) = b\underline{o}(a\underline{o}c)$ and so forth for all six possible combinations.

at the starting point at the completion of the fourth move. One might, therefore, say that there is changeability in process, but invariance in outcome.

c. A group contains an *identity* member such that its combination with any other member gives that other member, which means that it maintains that other member's identity. For instance, in groups whose rule of combination is additive, the identity member is zero (e.g., $5 + 0 = 5$); in groups whose combination rule is multiplication, the identity member is one, since any entity multiplied by one remains itself. If the totality of all sounds were a group, its identity member would be silence; while the identity member of the group of all changes of positions (i.e., of movements) would be immobility.

The concept of the identity member may at first sight appear specious. But it must be viewed as a special case of group invariance. Its practical importance has, for instance, been shown by Ashby (10, 11) for cybernetic systems, in which what he calls the null-function of the group of parametric changes plays a direct role in the maintenance of the stability of such systems. In relation to our concerns the point is that a member may act without making a difference.

d. Finally, in any system satisfying the group concept, we find that every member has its reciprocal or opposite, such that the combination of any member with its opposite gives the identity member; e.g., $5 + (-5) = 0$ where the combination rule is addition. Again we see that on the one hand this combination produces a marked change, but that on the other hand this result is itself a member of the group (in the present example the positive and negative integers, including zero) and is thus contained within it.

It is our contention that the Theory of Groups, even in the primitive terms used here to describe its basic concepts (illustrating ways in which particular changes may make no difference in the group), provides a valid framework for thinking about the peculiar interdependence between persistence and change which we can observe in many practical instances where plus ça change, plus c'est la même chose.

What Group Theory apparently cannot give us is a model for those types of change which transcend a given system or frame of reference. It is at this point that we have to turn to the Theory of Logical Types.

This theory, too, begins with the concept of collections of "things" which are united by a specific characteristic common to all of them. As in Group Theory, the components of the totality are called *members*, while the totality itself is called *class* rather than group. One essential axiom of the Theory of Logical Types is that "whatever involves *all* of a collection must not be one of the collection," as Whitehead and Russell state it in their monumental work *Principia Mathematica* (101). It should be immediately obvious that mankind is the class of all individuals, but that it is not itself an individual. Any attempt to deal with the one in terms of the other is doomed to lead to nonsense and confusion. For example, the economic behavior of the population of a large city cannot be understood in terms of the behavior of one inhabitant multipled by, say, four million. This, incidentally, was precisely the mistake committed in the early days of economic theory and is now scornfully referred to as the Robinson Crusoe economic model. A population of four million is not just quantitatively but qualitatively different from an individual, because it involves systems of interaction among the individuals. Similarly, while the individual members of a species are usually endowed with very specific survival mechanisms, it is well known that the *entire* species may race headlong towards extinction—and the human species is probably no exception. Conversely, in totalitarian ideologies the individual is seen only as a member of a class and thus becomes totally unimportant and expendable, an ant in an anthill, or as Koestler has so aptly put it with reference to his fellow inmate Nicolás in the death row of a Spanish prison: "In this view Nicolás existed merely as a social abstraction, a mathematical unit, obtained by dividing a mass of ten thousand Militiamen by ten thousand" (61).

Outcomes of the kind mentioned are the result of ignoring the paramount distinction between member and class and the fact that a class cannot be a member of itself. In all our pursuits, but especially in research, we are constantly faced with the hierarchies of logical levels, so the dangers of level confusions and their puzzling consequences are ubiquitous. The phenomena of change are no exception, but this is much more difficult to see in the behavioral sciences than, for instance, in physics. As Bateson points out (20), the simplest and most familiar form of change is motion, namely a change of position. But motion can itself be subject to change, i.e., to acceleration or deceleration, and this is a change of change (or metachange) of position. Still one level higher there is change of acceleration (or of deceleration) which amounts to change of change of change (or metametachange) of position. Even we laymen can appreciate that these forms of motion are very different phenomena involving very different explanatory principles and very different mathematical methods for their computation.[4] It can also be seen that change always involves the next higher level: to proceed, for instance, from position to motion, a step *out of* the theoretical framework of position is necessary. *Within* that framework the concept of motion cannot be generated, let alone dealt with, and any attempt at ignoring this basic axiom of the Theory of Logical Types leads to paradoxical confusion. To exemplify this crucial point further:

Myriads of things can be expressed in a language, except statements referring to that language itself.[5] If we want to talk *about* a language, as linguists and semanticists have to, we need a

---

[4]For instance, the mathematical treatment of change of acceleration has confronted space scientists with formerly unheard-of theoretical problems.

[5]Analogously, the only thing that cannot be measured in the metric system is the standard meter in Paris, precisely because it is the basis of the entire system. (The fact that it has now been replaced by far more accurate standards, based on the wave length of light, does not change this essential paradox.)

metalanguage which, in turn, requires a metametalanguage for the expression of its own structure. Very much the same holds for the relation between signs and their meaning. As early as 1893 the German mathematician Frege pointed to the need for differentiating clearly "between the cases in which I am speaking about the sign *itself* and those in which I am speaking about *its meaning*. However pedantic this may seem, I nevertheless hold it to be necessary. It is remarkable how an inexact manner of speech or of writing . . . can eventually confuse thought, once this awareness [of its inexactitude] has vanished" (37).

Or take the analogous example: the term *method* denotes a scientific procedure; it is the specification of the steps which must be taken in a given order to achieve a given end. *Methodology*, on the other hand, is a concept of the next higher logical type, it is the philosophical study of the plurality of methods which are applied in the various scientific disciplines. It always has to do with the activity of acquiring knowledge, not with a specific investigation in particular. It is, therefore, a *meta*method and stands in the same logical relation to method as a class to one of its members. To confuse method with methodology would produce philosophical nonsense since, as Wittgenstein once said, "philosophical problems arise when language goes on a holiday" (107).

Unfortunately, natural language often makes a clear distinction between member and class difficult. "It is conceivable," writes Bateson, "that the same *words* might be used in describing both a class and its members and be true in both cases. The word wave is the name of a class of movements of particles. We can also say that the wave itself moves; but we shall be referring to a movement of a class of movements. Under friction, this metamovement will not lose velocity as would the movement of a particle" (19).

Another one of Bateson's favorite examples is that usually only a schizophrenic is likely to eat the menu card instead of the meal (and complain of its bad taste, we would add).

Yet another useful analogy is supplied by an automobile with a conventional shift gear. The performance of the engine can be changed in two very different ways: either through the gas pedal (by increasing or decreasing the supply of fuel to the cylinders), or by shifting gears. Let us strain the analogy just a little and say that in each gear the car has a certain range of "behaviors" (i.e., of power output and consequently of speed, acceleration, climbing capacity, etc.). *Within* that range (i.e., that class of behaviors), appropriate use of the gas pedal will produce the desired change in performance. But if the required performance falls *outside* this range, the driver must shift gears to obtain the desired change. Gear-shifting is thus a phenomenon of a higher logical type than giving gas, and it would be patently nonsensical to talk about the mechanics of complex gears in the language of the thermodynamics of fuel supply.

But the formulation that is perhaps most relevant to our subject matter is the one given by Ashby for the cybernetic properties of a machine with input: "It will be seen that the word 'change' if applied to such a machine can refer to two very different things. There is the change from state to state, . . . , which is the machine's behavior, and there is the change from transformation to transformation, . . . , which is *a change of its way of behaving,* and which occurs at the whim of the experimenter or some outside factor. The distinction is fundamental and must on no account be slighted" (13).[6] There are, then, two important conclusions to be drawn from the postulates of the Theory of Logical Types: 1) logical levels must be kept strictly apart to prevent paradox and confusion; and 2) going from one level to the next higher (i.e., from member to class) entails a shift, a jump, a discontinuity or transformation—in a word, a change—of the

---

[6]A particular way of behaving, in order to persist (i.e., remain stable), involves and indeed *requires* changes at some lower level. For instance, a bicycle rider must engage in constant small oscillatory steering movements to maintain his equilibrium and ride smoothly. If these movements were somehow impeded (e.g., by somebody grabbing the handlebars) the rider would immediately lose his balance and fall off.

greatest theoretical and (as we shall see in the next chapters) practical importance, for it provides a way *out of* a system.

To summarize what has been said so far: Group Theory gives us a framework for thinking about the kind of change that can occur within a system that itself stays invariant; the Theory of Logical Types is not concerned with what goes on inside a class, i.e., between its members, but gives us a frame for considering the relationship between member and class and the peculiar metamorphosis which is in the nature of shifts from one logical level to the next higher. If we accept this basic distinction between the two theories, it follows that there are two different types of change: one that occurs within a given system which itself remains unchanged, and one whose occurrence changes the system itself.[7] To exemplify this distinction in more behavioral terms: a person having a nightmare can do many things *in* his dream— run, hide, fight, scream, jump off a cliff, etc.—but no change from any one of these behaviors to another would ever terminate the nightmare. *We shall henceforth refer to this kind of change as first-order change.* The one way *out of* a dream involves a change from dreaming to waking. Waking, obviously, is no longer a part of the dream, but a change to an altogether different state. *This kind of change will from now on be referred to as second-order*

[7]The Greeks seem to have known only the first of the two. "Nothing comes into being or is destroyed. Rather, a thing is mixed with or separated from already existing things," asserts Anaxagoras in his seventeenth fragment. Similarly, for Aristotle change is the passage from potentiality to actuality. And he expressly rules out what we nowadays would call a shift from level to metalevel, when he writes: "There cannot be motion of motion, or becoming of becoming, or in general change of change" (9). The later Greeks and the Middle Ages tended to see change as the antinomy between being and becoming. Only Heraclitus, it appears, envisaged change in a different perspective. In addition to his well-known dictum about the impossibility of stepping into the same river twice, he asserts in another fragment: "All change is contradictory; therefore contradiction is the very essence of reality." The evolution of the concept of change is well summarized by Prior: "It would hardly be too much to say that modern science began when people became accustomed to the idea of changes changing, e.g. to the idea of acceleration as opposed to simple motion" (80).

change. (The equivalence of this distinction with Ashby's cybernetic definition of the two kinds of change, quoted earlier, is evident.) Second-order change is thus *change of change*—the very phenomenon whose existence Aristotle denied so categorically.

At this point of our inquiry we must retrace our steps and take another look at our very simplistic presentation of Group Theory. In the light of what we have now learned from the Theory of Logical Types, we realize that the four properties of any group that are responsible for creating the particular interdependence of persistence and change within the group are not themselves members of the group. They are clearly about, and therefore *meta* to, the group. This becomes particularly evident with reference to the combination rules holding for a particular group. We saw, for instance, that where the internal group operations are effected by the rule of multiplication, the identity member is 1. If the combination rule in this group were changed to addition (a second-order change that could only be introduced from the outside and could not be generated from within the group), there would be a different outcome: member n combined with the identity member (1) would no longer be itself (as it would be under the old rule, where n multiplied by one would again give n), but we would obtain $n + 1$. We can now appreciate that groups are invariant only on the first-order change level (i.e., on the level of change from one member to another, where, indeed, the more things change, the more they remain the same), but are open to change on the second-order change level (i.e., to changes in the body of rules governing their structure or internal order). Group Theory and the Theory of Logical Types thus reveal themselves not only as compatible with each other, but also as complementary. Furthermore (and bearing in mind that when we talk about change in connection with problem formation and problem resolution we always mean second-order change), we find that the two theories equip us with a conceptual framework useful in examining concrete, practical examples of change. And finally, remembering that second-order change is always in the nature of a discontinuity or a logical jump, we may expect the practical manifestations of second-order change to appear as illogical and paradoxical as the decision of the commandant of the castle of Hochosterwitz to throw away his last food in order to survive.

2
THE PRACTICAL PERSPECTIVE

I would not dream of belonging to a club that is willing to have me for a member.

—GROUCHO MARX

WHILE it is relatively easy to establish a clear distinction between first-order change and second-order change in strictly theoretical terms, this same distinction can be extremely difficult to make in real-life situations. Thus, inattention to this difference and confusion between the two levels of change can occur very easily, and actions may be taken in difficult situations which not only do not produce the desired change, but compound the problem to which the "solution" is applied. However, before dealing with solutions, practical examples for the theoretical considerations contained in Chapter 1 are needed.

a. It is not difficult to find examples for the first group property (that any combination, transformation, or operation of group members gives again a group member, and thus maintains the group structure). In John Fowles' novel *The Collector*, a young man has abducted the beautiful art student Miranda, with whom he is in love, and is holding her prisoner in a remote and escape-proof house in the country. Although she is completely in his power, the situation that he has created makes him as much her prisoner as she is his. Because he hopes desperately that she will eventually begin to love him, he can neither coerce nor release her. Release is out of the question for practical reasons also: he would be arrested for a serious crime, unless, of course, she were to claim that she followed him voluntarily. She is willing to promise this, but he knows that this would at best be a ruse to obtain her freedom and that she would never return to him. Under these unusual circumstances, both she and he are desperately attempting to effect a change (he by trying to make her love him, she by trying to escape), but any move by either of them is of the first-order change type and so consolidates and compounds the impasse.

A similar situation arises in the film *Knife in the Water*. A married couple pick up a hitchhiker and take him along on their sailing trip. Tension and jealousy soon build up between the two men, each of whom is insecure and wants to impress the pretty wife at the other's expense. They finally come to blows: the young man (who had earlier mentioned that he cannot swim) falls overboard and disappears. The husband dives after him, cannot find him, and finally swims ashore to alert the police, while the young man (who had only been hiding behind a buoy) returns to the boat, seduces the wife, and then leaves as they reach the yacht harbor. The husband returns; he was unable to turn himself in but is equally unable to reconcile himself to the thought of having caused the other's death. The wife, of course, tells him that the young man is alive, but the husband is convinced that she is only trying to set his mind at ease. Seeing all her attempts at resolving the impasse fail, she eventually uses what she believes to be her most powerful and convincing argument, and tells him the whole truth: "He is not only alive, he also made me unfaithful to you." This "solution" not only does not produce the hoped-for change but actually precludes it: if he ever were to believe that he did not kill the other man, it would be at the price of believing that she had indeed betrayed him; but if she was not unfaithful, then he has killed the other man.

Two other examples, mentioned elsewhere, fall into the same category and shall be repeated here briefly: The constitution of an imaginary country provides for unlimited parliamentary debate. This rule can be used to paralyze democratic procedure completely—the opposition party only has to engage in endless speeches to make impossible any decision that is not to its liking. To escape this impasse, a change of the rule is absolutely necessary, but can be made impossible precisely by what is to be changed, i.e. by endless filibuster (98). That this example is not merely intellectual exercise, but has very practical analogies in the world of international relations, is shown by the other example, a quotation from Osgood: "Our political and military leaders have been virtually unanimous in public assertions that we must go ahead and stay ahead in the armament race; they have been equally unanimous in saying nothing about what happens then. Suppose we achieve the state of ideal mutual deterrence . . . what then? Surely no sane man can envisage our planet spinning on into eternity, divided into two armed camps poised to destroy each other, and call it peace and security! *The point is that the policy of mutual deterrence includes no provisions for its own resolution* (77)." This last sentence points very clearly to the invariance factor which prevents a system (this term is being used here as equivalent to *group* in the mathematical sense) from generating within itself the conditions for second-order change. It can, as we have seen, run through many first-order change phenomena, but as its structure remains invariant, there is no second-order change.

b. Group property *b*, it will be remembered, has to do with the fact that a sequence of operations, performed on the group members in accordance with the combination rule of that group, may be changed without changing the result of the operations. A rather abstract example has been given in Chapter 1. More directly related to our subject matter are examples which can be found in the functioning of complex homeostatic systems. These systems may run through long sequences of internal states—and even over long periods of observation no two such sequences need to be exactly alike—but eventually reach the same result, i.e., their steady state. Ashby's homeostat (10) is a model of this. In the realm of human interaction, a pattern frequently observed is that involving two partners, e.g., two spouses, who for one reason or another maintain a certain emotional distance between each other. In this system it does not matter if either tries to establish more contact, for every advance by one partner is predictably and observably followed by a withdrawal of the other, so that the overall pattern is at all times preserved.[1] A somewhat more complex pattern of essentially the same structure is often found when a drinker provokes criticism and surveillance of his drinking by his wife. As she complains and attempts to "protect" him from alcohol, his drinking increases, which, in turn, brings about an increase in her criticism, etc. Similarly, when a juvenile delinquent's behavior improves, his parents may "discover" delinquent behavior in a child previously regarded as the "good one." This is not just their fantasy; clinical experience shows that, indeed, this so-called counter-delinquent's behavior can often be seen to undergo marked changes as soon as his sibling "goes straight." Instead of being critical of his sibling's badness, as before, he may now taunt him for his goodness and thereby either re-establish the original situation or engage in delinquency himself. Similar patterns can be observed in the decision-making of certain families. When they are trying to plan something together, it does not matter who proposes something, the others are bound to dismiss the idea. A particularly interesting clinical example was mentioned to us recently by Professor Selvini Palazzoli from her work with numerous Italian families with anorectic daughters. Almost all these girls, although abhorring food themselves, showed an

---

[1] The patent lawfulness of their behavior has prompted one of us (R.F.) to speculate that they appear to be joined (and kept apart) by an invisible ten-foot pole attached to their waists, so that every attempt by one partner to come closer pushes the other away, and vice versa, giving rise to endless mutual accusations, but resulting in a wondrous dance in which nothing ever changes.

inordinate interest in cooking and in supplying food to the rest of their family. The overall impression, as Selvini puts it, is that in these families there is an extreme, almost caricaturing reversal of the function of feeder and fed. Such sequences of behaviors, maintaining what Jackson called family homeostasis (49, 50), are not just role reversals, as the sociologist may conceptualize them, but true first-order change phenomena, whereby different behaviors out of a finite repertory of possible behaviors are combined into different sequences, but leading to identical outcomes.

In general, the persistence phenomena inherent in group property b can be observed most frequently wherever the causality of a sequence is circular rather than linear, which is usual in ongoing systems of interacting elements. Armaments races and escalations, like that between the Arab countries and Israel, are good examples. Assuming for simplicity's sake that there are only two parties involved, the circularity of their interaction makes it undecidable for all practical purposes whether a given action is the cause or the effect of an action by the other party. Individually, of course, either party sees its actions as determined and provoked by the other's actions; but seen from the outside, as a whole, any action by either partner is a stimulus, provoking a reaction, which reaction is then itself again a stimulus for what the other part considers "merely" a reaction. Within this frame, behavior b applied to behavior a is practically equivalent to the application of a to b, which satisfies the second group property where, as we have seen, $a \circ b = b \circ a$. Discrepancies in the way the participants in an interaction "punctuate" the sequence of events can become the cause of serious conflict (17, 67, 93).

c. The identity member, which is the basis of group property c, means, in essence, *zero first-order change* when combined with any other member. This complicates exemplification, for it is difficult to show that which is *not* the case, or trivial to emphasize that anything that does not produce change leaves things as they are. But this is only apparently so; it ceases to be trivial the moment we realize that zero change refers of necessity to both levels of change. However, for the moment it may be simplest to proceed to exemplifications of the last group property, for in the course of this it will become easier to appreciate that the identity member is not just a *nothing*, but has substance of its own.

d. Group property *d*, as we have seen, refers to the fact that the combination of any group member with its reciprocal or opposite gives the identity member. What are the practical implications of this postulate? On the surface it would be difficult to imagine a more drastic and radical change than the replacement of something by its opposite. But in a somewhat less superficial perspective it quickly becomes apparent that the world of our experience (which is all we can talk about) is made up of pairs of opposites and that, strictly speaking, any aspect of reality derives its substance or concreteness from the existence of its opposite. Examples are numerous and commonplace: light and dark, figure and ground, good and evil, past and future, and many, many other such pairs are merely the two complementary aspects of one and the same reality or frame of reference, their seemingly incompatible and mutually exclusive nature notwithstanding.[2] To exemplify:

[2]Cf. Lao-tzu: Under Heaven all can see beauty only as beauty because there is ugliness. All can know good as good only because there is evil (69, Chapter 2).

This interdependence between a group member and its reciprocal is well borne out by the peculiar crisis that occurs when for one reason or another the one is no longer counterbalanced by the other, desirable as this may seem at first glance. Only then can the stabilizing function of this interdependence be appreciated, a fact that can again and again be observed in family therapy. If and when the condition of the identified patient (the family member who carries the official label of a psychiatric diagnosis) improves, there usually is no great rejoicing; either the family system attempts to lead the "patient" back into his scapegoat function (most frequently by defining any improvement as new evidence of his craziness), or another family member may become the identified patient. Unpleasant as it may be in and by itself, an unresolved dilemma can very well be a kind of solution, as Constantinos Cavafy masterfully sketches this in his poem "Expecting the Barbarians": Rome is awaiting the invasion of the barbarians; the emperor, senators, consuls, and pretors are assembled to receive them at the gates; life in the city has almost come to a standstill, for once the barbarians are here, everything will be different—and then:

One of the changes effected by the Red Guards during the early stages of the Chinese Cultural Revolution was the destruction of all public signs (of streets, shops, buildings, etc.) which contained any reference to the reactionary, "bourgeois" past, and their replacement by revolutionary names. Could there be a more radical break with the past? But in the wider context of Chinese culture this break is fully in keeping with that basic rule which Confucius called the *rectification of names* and which is based on the belief that from the "right" name the "right" reality should follow—rather than assuming, as we do in the West, that names *reflect* reality. In effect, therefore, the renaming imposed by the Red Guards was of the first-order change type; it not only left an age-old feature of Chinese culture intact, but actually re-emphasized it. Thus there was no second-order change involved, a fact that the Red Guards would probably have had difficulty appreciating.

Things may be "as different as day and night" and the change from the one to the other appear to be extreme and ultimate, and yet, paradoxically, in the wider context (within the group in the mathematical sense) nothing may have changed at all. "In order to save the town we had to destroy it," an American field commander in Vietnam is supposed to have said, presumably unaware of both the dreadful absurdity and the deeper meaning of his report. One of the most common fallacies about change is the conclusion that if something is bad, its opposite must of necessity be good. The woman who divorces a "weak" man in order to

---

Why this sudden unrest and confusion?
(How solemn their faces have become.)
Why are the streets and squares clearing quickly,
and all return to their homes, so deep in thought?

Because night is here but the barbarians have not come.
Some people arrived from the frontiers,
and they said that there are no longer any barbarians.
And now what shall become of us without any barbarians?
Those people were a kind of solution.

marry a "strong" one often discovers to her dismay that while her second marriage should be the exact opposite of the first, nothing much has actually changed. The invocation of stark contrast has always been a favorite propaganda technique of politicians and dictators. "National Socialism or Bolshevik chaos?" pompously asked a Nazi poster, implying that there were only these two alternatives and that all men of good will should make the obvious choice. "Erdäpfel oder Kartoffel?" (Spuds or Potatoes?) read a little sticker which an underground group affixed to hundreds of these posters, triggering off a huge Gestapo investigation.

This strange interdependence of opposites was already known to Heraclitus, the great philosopher of change, who called it *enantiodromia.* The concept was taken up by C. G. Jung, who saw in it a fundamental psychic mechanism: "Every psychological extreme secretly contains its own opposite or stands in some sort of intimate and essential relation to it. . . . There is no hallowed custom that cannot on occasion turn into its opposite and the more extreme a position is, the more easily may we expect an enantiodromia, a conversion of something into its opposite" (53). Our history is certainly rich in enantiodromic patterns. For instance, when Hellenism reached its most rarefied spirituality, there followed an irruption of dark, chaotic, orphic elements from Asia Minor. The romantic idealization of women in the troubadour era of the eleventh to thirteenth centuries and its religious counterpart, the fervent cult of the Virgin Mary from the eleventh century onwards, had a strange, terrifying fellow traveler through history: the outbreak and the horrible crescendo of the witch hunts. Mary and the witch—two aspects of femininity which could hardly be more antithetical and apart; and yet they are "only" a pair of opposites.[3] Later, in the Age of Enlightenment, we see the Virgin replaced by the goddess Reason, who is

[3]In Hinduism this pair of opposites is much more appropriately represented as *one* divinity, the goddess Kali, who creates *and* destroys.

in turn dethroned by Romanticism and the "discovery" of the unconscious by C. G. Carus. And, to cast a brief glance into the future, it is a fairly safe bet that the offspring of our contemporary hippie generation will want to become bank managers and will despise communes, leaving their well-meaning but bewildered parents with the nagging question: Where did we fail our children?

With these examples in mind, the concept of the identity member should become a little less elusive. As pointed out under c) above, combined with a group member it preserves the identity of *that member* (i.e., produces zero first-order change), while the combination of a group member with its opposite preserves the identity of the *group* (i.e., produces the identity member and therefore zero second-order change). For example: It is in the nature of tradition to ensure persistence, if necessary through corrective action. As a basis for action, tradition can, therefore, be considered as having the function of an identity member. On the other hand, it is in the nature of revolution to bring about change. But as the Red Guard example shows, there can be revolutionary action which is itself a traditional way of attempting change. This type of action has thus the function of a reciprocal or opposite and, as we have seen, preserves the identity of a social system. In fact, history offers an embarrassingly long list of revolutions whose end results were, by and large, more of the same conditions which the revolution had set out to overthrow and replace by a brave new world.[4] In everyday human affairs, the

---

[4]With his astute intuition Dostoyevsky caricatures this vicious circle in *The Possessed.* Addressing a group of conspirators is Shigalov, the author of an enormously complex "study of the social organization which is in the future to replace the present condition of things" and which will guarantee complete freedom. He is willing to explain his thoughts in abbreviated form, but this will "occupy at least ten evening sessions, one for each of my chapters." (There was the sound of laughter.) "I must add, besides, that my system is not yet complete." (Laughter again.) "I am perplexed by my own data, and my conclusion is in direct contradiction to the original idea with which I started. Starting from unlimited freedom, I arrived at unlimited despotism. I will add, however, that there can be no other solution of the social formula than mine." (The laughter grew.)" (28).

eventual recognition of this zero change may then lead cooler heads to the sad conclusion: We would probably have been better off not bothering with the situation in the first place. But this realization is by no means the rule; more often than not the peculiar "zero" effect of the identity member is all the greater because of its "invisibility." It is one thing to notice, take into account, or argue about something as patent as a change of something into its opposite, but it is very difficult, especially in human relationships, to be aware that this change actually is no change in the overall pattern. Much human conflict and many conflict-engendering "solutions" are due to this unawareness. Additional examples will be presented in Chapter 4.

So much for our exemplifications of the four group properties. They show us that any one, or any combination, of these properties cannot produce second-order change. A system which may run through all its possible internal changes (no matter how many there are) without effecting a systemic change, i.e., second-order change, is said to be caught in a *Game Without End* (97). It cannot generate from within itself the conditions for its own change; it cannot produce the rules for the change of its own rules. Admittedly, there are games which have their end point built into their structure, and they will reach it sooner or later. Whether these outcomes are happy or painful, such games do not lead into the vicious circles which are almost invariably found at the roots of human conflict. Games without end are precisely what the name implies: they are endless in the sense that they contain no provisions for their own termination. Termination (like waking up, in our nightmare example) is not part of the game, is not a member of that group; termination is *meta* to the game, is of a different logical type than any move (any first-order change) within the game.

Yet there is the undeniable fact that far from being impossible, second-order change is an everyday phenomenon: people *do* find new solutions, social organisms *are* capable of self-correction, nature finds ever-new adaptations, and the whole process of scientific discovery or artistic creation is based precisely on the stepping out of an old into a new framework—in fact, the most useful criterion for judging the viability or "health" of a system is exactly this puzzling, uncommonsense ability which Baron Münchhausen demonstrated when he pulled himself from the quagmire by his own pigtail.

But the occurrence of second-order change is ordinarily viewed as something uncontrollable, even incomprehensible, a quantum jump, a sudden illumination which unpredictably comes at the end of long, often frustrating mental and emotional labor, sometimes in a dream, sometimes almost as an act of grace in the theological sense. Koestler, in his *Act of Creation*, has collected an encyclopedic array of examples of this phenomenon, and has introduced the concept of *bisociation*. According to him, bisociation is "the perceiving of a situation or idea in two self-consistent but habitually incompatible frames of reference" (59), and "the sudden bisociation of a mental event with two habitually incompatible matrices results in an abrupt transfer of the train of thought from one associative context to another" (60). In a brilliant paper, Bronowski deals with the same problem and also assigns to the decisive leap an unpredictable, almost random nature: we do not know how this event occurs, and there is no way in which we can know it. "It is a free play of the mind, an invention outside the logical processes. This is the central act of imagination in science, and it is in all respects like any similar act in literature. In this respect, science and literature are alike: in both of them, the mind decides to enrich the system as it stands by an addition which is made by an unmechanical act of free choice" (27).

Despite such combined weight of authority and common perception, it is our experience that second-order change appears unpredictable, abrupt, illogical etc. only in terms of first-order change, that is, from within the system.[5] Indeed, this must be so, because, as we have seen, second-order change is introduced into the system from the outside and therefore is not something familiar or something understandable in terms of the vicissitudes of first-order change. Hence its puzzling, seemingly capricious nature. But seen from outside the system, it merely amounts to a change of the premises (the combination rules in terms of Group Theory) governing the system *as a whole*. No doubt this group of premises may itself again be subject to group invariance, and any change of these premises would then have to be introduced from a yet higher level (i.e., one that is *meta-meta* to the original system and *meta* to the premises governing that system as a whole). However—and this is an eminently practical and crucial point—to effect change within the original system it is sufficient to go only as far as the metalevel.

A somewhat abstract but very simple example will make this clearer. The nine dots shown in Figure 1 are to be connected by four straight lines without lifting the pencil from the paper. The reader who is not familiar with this problem is advised to stop at this point and to try the solution on a piece of paper before reading on, and especially before turning to the solution (Figure 2) on page 27.

[5]Since 1931, when Gödel published his famous undecidability theorem (41), using *Principia Mathematica* as his basis, we may safely abandon the hope that any system complex enough to include arithmetic (or, as Tarski (88) has shown, any language of that complexity) will ever be able to prove its consistency within its own framework. This proof can only come from the outside, based on additional axioms, premises, concepts, comparisons, etc., which the original system itself cannot generate or prove, and which are themselves again only provable by recourse to a yet wider framework, and so on in an infinite regress of metasystems, metametasystems, etc. In keeping with the basic postulates of *Principia Mathematica*, any statement *about* a collection (and the proof of consistency is one such statement) involves all of the collection and cannot, must not, therefore, be part of it.

• • •

• • •

• • •

Figure 1

Almost everybody who first tries to solve this problem introduces as part of his problem-solving an assumption which makes the solution impossible. The assumption is that the dots compose a square and that the solution must be found *within* that square, a self-imposed condition which the instructions do not contain. His failure, therefore, does not lie in the impossibility of the task, but in his attempted solution. Having now created the problem, it does not matter in the least which combination of four lines he now tries, and in what order; he always finishes with at least one unconnected dot. This means that he can run through the totality of the first-order change possibilities existing within the square but will never solve the task. The solution is a second-order change which consists in leaving the field and which cannot be contained within itself because, in the language of *Principia Mathematica*, it involves all of a collection and cannot, therefore, be part of it.[6]

Very few people manage to solve the nine-dot problem by themselves. Those who fail and give up are usually surprised at the unexpected simplicity of the solution (see Figure 2). The analogy

[6]To give two other illustrations of this crucial distinction between "inside" and "outside": One cannot obtain full visual perception of one's own body (at least not directly), because the eyes, as the perceiving organs, are themselves part of the totality to be perceived, or, as a Zen master put it, "Life is a sword that wounds, but cannot wound itself; like an eye that sees, but cannot see itself." For the same reason, it is extremely difficult to arrive at a more than superficial understanding of one's own culture; one has to leave it and then be prepared for a shock when looking at it from the outside (i.e., from the vantage-point of another culture), as all anthropologists and many Peace Corps volunteers know.

between this and many a real-life situation is obvious. We have all found ourselves caught in comparable boxes, and it did not matter whether we tried to find the solution calmly and logically or, as is more likely, ended up running frantically around in circles. But, as mentioned already, it is only from inside the box, in the first-order change perspective, that the solution appears as a surprising flash of enlightenment beyond our control. In the second-order change perspective it is a simple change from one set of premises to another of the same logical type. The one set includes the rule that the task must be solved within the (assumed) square; the other does not. In other words, the solution is found as a result of examining the assumptions *about* the dots, not the dots themselves.[7] Or, to make the same statement in more philosophical terms, it obviously makes a difference whether we consider ourselves as pawns in a game whose rules we call reality or as players of the game who know that the rules are "real" only to the extent that we have created or accepted them, and that we can change them. We shall return to this subject in greater detail in Chapter 8.

[7]At this point it may be useful to compare this kind of problem-solving and change with the assumptions that are at the root of most classical schools of psychotherapy. It is generally held that change comes about through insight into the past causes which are responsible for the present trouble. But, as the nine-dot problem exemplifies, there is no cogent reason for this excursion into the past; the genesis of the self-defeating assumption which precludes the solution is quite irrelevant, the problem is solved in the here and now by stepping outside the "box." There is increasing awareness among clinicians that while insight may provide very sophisticated *explanations* of a symptom, it does little if anything to change it for the better.

This empirical fact raises an important epistemological issue. All theories have limitations which follow logically from their premises. In the case of psychiatric theories, these limitations are more often than not attributed to human nature. For instance, within the psychoanalytic framework, symptom removal without the solution of the underlying conflict responsible for the symptom *must* lead to symptom substitution. This is not because this complication lies in the nature of the human *mind;* it lies in the nature of the *theory,* i.e., in the conclusions that logically follow from its premises. The behavior therapists, on the other hand, base themselves on learning and extinction theories and therefore need not worry about the dreaded consequences of symptom removal.

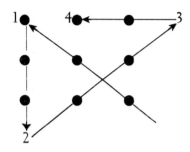

Figure 2. *The solution of the nine-dot problem.*

But all of this presupposes awareness of the logical structure of our universe and of the need to keep the levels of logical discourse neatly separated. The Theory of Logical Types makes it clear that we must not talk about the class in the language appropriate for its members. This would be an error in logical typing and would lead to the very perplexing impasses of logical paradox. Such errors of typing can occur in two ways: either by incorrectly ascribing a particular property to the class instead of to the member (or vice versa), or by neglecting the paramount distinction between class and member and by treating the two as if they were of the same level of abstraction. It will be remembered that second-order change is of the next-higher logical level, the $(n + 1)$th level, than first-order change. It cannot, therefore, be expressed in the language appropriate to first-order change or achieved by the methods applicable to the first-order change level without causing the most perplexing, paradoxical consequences.[8] For instance, some of the tragicomic controversies between experimental psychologists and psychiatrists could be avoided if they realized that when the former talk about change, they usually

---

[8]Most forms of humor are based on the deliberate confusion between member and class; Groucho Marx's statement, the epigraph to this chapter, is a classical example. For an extensive treatment of this subject see Fry (38).

mean first-order change (i.e., a change from one behavior to another within a given way of behaving), while psychiatrists, though often not aware of this, are predominantly concerned with second-order change (i.e., the change from one way of behaving to another). Bateson, whose greatest contribution to the behavioral sciences probably is precisely the introduction of the Theory of Logical Types into the field, and whose mentorship we gratefully acknowledge, summarized this state of affairs succinctly when he stated: "Insofar as behavioral scientists still ignore the problems of *Principia Mathematica*, they can claim approximately sixty years of obsolescence" (18).

PART TWO
Problem Formation

3

"MORE OF THE SAME" OR, WHEN THE SOLUTION BECOMES THE PROBLEM

We first raise the dust and then claim we cannot see.
—BERKELEY

Now that you have broken through the wall with your head, what will you do in the neighbouring cell?
—S. J. LEC, *New Unkempt Thoughts*

ORDINARILY, the promoter of change (even in certain aspects of growth and development) is deviance from some norm. When winter comes and the temperature begins to fall, rooms must be heated and one must wear warm clothing outside in order to remain comfortable. If the temperature falls even lower, more heat and warm clothing are needed. In other words, change becomes necessary to re-establish the norm, both for comfort and survival. The desired change is achieved through applying the opposite of what produced the deviance (e.g., heat vs. cold) in accordance with group property *d*. Should this corrective action be insufficient, *more of the same* eventually achieves the desired effect. This simple and "logical" type of problem solving not only applies to many situations in everyday life, but is at the root of myriads of interactive processes in physiology, neurology, physics, economics, and many other fields.

Nevertheless, this is not the whole story. Let us consider some other, ostensibly similar, situations. Alcoholism is a serious social problem. Restrictions must therefore be placed on the consumption of alcohol, and when this does not eliminate the problem, more of the same is carried to its ultimate—prohibition. But prohibition as the cure of this social evil turns out to be worse than the disease: alcoholism rises, a whole clandestine industry comes into existence, the low quality of its products makes alcohol into even more of a public health problem, a special police force is needed to hunt down the bootleggers and in the process becomes unusually corrupt, etc., etc. As the problem thus worsens, the enforcement of prohibition is made more stringent, but here *more of the same* "surprisingly" does not produce the desired change. On the contrary, the "solution" greatly contributes to the problem—in fact, it eventually becomes the greater of the two evils (i.e., a certain percentage of alcoholics in the general population on the one hand, and widespread smuggling, corruption, and gangland warfare *in addition* to a high rate of alcoholism on the other).

This example also serves to illustrate another important and at first glance contradictory point about change in real-life situations. In the abstract terms of Group Theory, the members of a group (e.g., integers, particles) are conceived of as unchanging in their individual properties; what may undergo considerable change is their sequence, their relations to each other, and so on. In real life, although some human problems may continue at a steady level of severity, many difficulties do not stay the same for long, but tend to increase and escalate if no solution or a wrong solution is attempted—and especially if *more* of a wrong solution is applied. When this happens, the situation may remain structurally similar or identical, but the intensity of the difficulty and of the suffering entailed increases. The reader should bear this distinction in mind, for otherwise our next examples may seem to contain a contradiction: namely, that on the one hand the problem is presented as remaining unchanged, while on the other it is described as getting steadily worse.

Is pornography a pernicious social evil? For many people the answer is an unquestionable (and unquestioned) yes. It is therefore logical to fight and repress pornography by all available legal means. But the Danish example has shown that the complete liberalization of pornography has not only not opened the floodgates of sin and general depravity, but has actually made people ridicule and ignore it.[1] In the case of pornography, then, the "more of the same" solution (legal repression) is not just the greater of two problems, it *is* the problem, for without the "solution" there would be no problem.

It is odd to see how on the one hand the absurdity of this type of solution becomes patent, while on the other hand this form of change is attempted again and again, as if those responsible for bringing about change were unable to draw the necessary conclusions from history.[2] The generation gap can be taken as another example. This painful friction between the older and the younger generations has evidently existed for a very long time and has been lamented in remarkably stereotypical terms throughout the millenia.[3] But age-old as this nuisance is, nobody seems to have found a way of changing it, and there is thus reason to assume that it has no solution. Nowadays, however, a sufficiently large number of people have convinced themselves that the generation gap can and must be closed. *This conviction,* not the generation gap, creates untold problems—mainly through an increased polarization between the generations—where formerly there was only a difficulty with which mankind had apparently learned to live. But

[1]Admittedly, at the time of this writing the Danish smut factories are still working overtime, but their output goes almost exclusively into those countries whose citizens are still "protected" by law against it.

[2]For instance, the dismal failure of the U.S. experiment with prohibition did not prevent the Republic of India, fourteen years after the U.S. repeal, from writing prohibition into her constitution, and from running into exactly the same problems.

[3]A Babylonian clay tablet whose age has been estimated to be at least three thousand years reads: "Today's youth is rotten to the core, it is evil, godless, and lazy. It will never be what youth used to be, and it will never be able to preserve our culture."

having now increased an incipient polarization, more and more people begin to "see" that more needs to be done. "More of the same" is their recipe for change, and this "solution" is the problem.

We take the view that the same complication is involved in many refractory human problems where common sense would suggest that the way to counteract a painful or disturbing fact is by introducing its opposite into the situation. For instance, what could seem more reasonable to relatives and friends than to try to cheer up a depressed person? But in all likelihood the depressed person not only does not benefit from this, but sinks deeper into gloom. This then prompts the others to increase their efforts to make him see the silver lining in every cloud. Guided by "reason" and "common sense," they are unable to see (and the patient is unable to say) that what their help amounts to is a demand that the patient have certain feelings (joy, optimism, etc.) and not others (sadness, pessimism, etc.). As a result, what for the patient might originally only have been a temporary sadness now becomes infused with feelings of failure, badness, and ingratitude toward those who love him so much and are trying so hard to help him. *This* then is the depression—not the original sadness. The pattern can be observed most frequently in families where the parents so firmly subscribe to the idea that a well brought-up child should be a happy child that they will see a silent imputation in even the most normal, temporary mood of sadness or crankiness of their child, and the "sadness equals badness" equation is thereby established. The command, "Go to your room and don't come out until you have a smile on your face" is then just one of many similar ways in which the parents may try to bring about a change. The child's mood is now not only one of guilt for being unable to feel what he "should" feel in order to be acceptable and "good," but presumably also one of impotent rage at what is being done to him—two more feelings which the parents can then add to the list of those which he should not have. Once this pattern of mishandling a basically harmless difficulty has been set and has become a habitual expectation, the outside reinforcement (here the parental attempts at bringing about change) is no longer necessary. Clinical experience shows that the individual will eventually apply the depression-engendering "solution" to himself and thereby become fit to be labeled a patient.

An essentially identical, counterproductive form of problem solving is usually attempted by a person who has difficulty falling asleep—a common albeit upsetting trouble known at some time to virtually everybody. The mistake most insomniacs make is to try to force themselves somehow to achieve sleep by an act of will power—only to find that they stay wide awake. Sleep is by its very nature a phenomenon which can occur only spontaneously. It cannot occur spontaneously when it is willed. But the insomniac who is increasingly desperate with the ticking away of time is doing just this, and his attempted "cure" eventually becomes his disease. "More of the same" may here lead to dietary changes, alterations in his bedtime scheduling, sleeping medication, and consequent drug dependence; and each of these steps, rather than solving his problem, intensifies it.

In marriage therapy, one can frequently see both spouses engaging in behaviors which they individually consider the most appropriate reaction to something wrong that the other is doing. That is, in the eyes of each of them the particular corrective behavior of the other is seen as that behavior which needs correction. For instance, a wife may have the impression that her husband is not open enough for her to know where she stands with him, what is going on in his head, what he is doing when he is away from home, etc. Quite naturally, she will therefore attempt to get the needed information by asking him questions, watching his behavior, and checking on him in a variety of other ways. If he considers her behavior as too intrusive, he is likely to withhold from her information which in and by itself would be quite harmless and irrelevant to disclose—"just to teach her that she need not know everything." Far from making her back down, this attempted solution not only does not bring about the desired change in her behavior but provides further fuel for her worries and her distrust—"if he does not even talk to me about these little things, there *must* be something the matter." The less information he gives her, the more persistently she will seek it, and the more she seeks it, the less he will give her. By the time they see a psychiatrist, it will be tempting to diagnose her behavior as pathological jealousy—provided that no attention is paid to their pattern of interaction and their attempted solutions, which *are* the problem.

What all of the above examples show is that under certain circumstances problems will arise purely as the result of wrong attempts at changing an existing difficulty,[4] and that this kind of problem formation may arise on any level of human functioning —individual, dyadic, familial, sociopolitical, etc. In the case of the two spouses just mentioned, the observer is left with the impression of two sailors hanging out of either side of a sailboat in order to steady it: the more the one leans overboard, the more the other has to hang out to compensate for the instability created by the other's attempts at stabilizing the boat, while the boat itself would be quite steady if not for their acrobatic efforts at steadying it (see Figure 3). It is not difficult to see that in order to change this absurd situation, at least one of them has to do something seemingly quite unreasonable, namely to "steady" *less* and not more, since this will immediately force the other to also do less of the same (unless he wants to finish up in the water), and they may eventually find themselves comfortably back inside a steady boat. This uncommonsense way of effecting change will be the subject matter of Chapter 7; let us conclude this chapter by showing how the above examples fit into our theory of change.

As the first example (heat vs. cold) illustrates, there indeed exist

---

[4]Or, more absurdly still, even a nonexistent difficulty, as will be shown in Chapter 5.

Figure 3. *Two sailors frantically steadying a (steady) boat*

countless situations in which a deviation from a norm can be changed back to normal through the application of its opposite. In terms of cybernetic theory, this is a simple negative feedback phenomenon[5] by which a system regains and maintains its internal stability. In terms of Group Theory this homeostatic process has the fourth group property in that its outcome is the identity member, or zero change. As already mentioned, there are countless instances in which this form of problem solving and change provides a valid and satisfactory solution. In all these cases the first-order change potential inherent in the system can cope with the disturbance, and the system's structure remains unchanged.

All the other examples presented in this chapter illustrate cases in which first-order change, regardless of which of the four group properties is involved, is incapable of effecting the desired change, because here the system's structure itself has to undergo change, and this can be effected only from the second-order change level. (In terms of our automobile example, this means that one has to shift gears rather than push the gas pedal down to the floorboard; in terms of cybernetic theory it means that a step-functional change has to occur.) The attempt to effect a first-order change under these circumstances either greatly contributes to the problem which it is supposed to solve, or actually *is* the problem.

At the risk of seeming to engage in semantic hair-splitting, we must at this point draw a clear distinction between our use of the terms *difficulties* and *problems*. When in the following we speak about difficulties, we shall simply mean an undesirable state of affairs which either can be resolved through some common-sense action (usually of the first-order change type, e.g., heat vs. cold) for which no special problem solving skills are necessary, or, more

---

[5]For the reader unfamiliar with cybernetic terminology, we should point out that "negative feedback" refers to the opposite or the converse (and thus the cancellation) of an existing deviation. It is not a value judgment and should *not* be understood in its colloquial, but erroneous, usage, e.g., "The speaker got a lot of negative feedback," meaning that his audience disagreed with him.

frequently, we shall mean an undesirable but usually quite common life situation for which there exists no known solution and which—at least for the time being— must simply be lived with. We shall talk about problems when referring to impasses, deadlocks, knots, etc., which are created and maintained through the mishandling of difficulties. There are basically three ways in which this mishandling can occur:

A. A solution is attempted by denying that a problem is a problem; *action is necessary, but is not taken.*

B. Change is attempted regarding a difficulty which for all practical purposes is either unchangeable (e.g., the generation gap, or a certain percentage of incurable alcoholics in the general population) or nonexistent; *action is taken when it should not be.*

C. An error in logical typing is committed and a Game Without End established. This may occur either by attempting a first-order change in a situation which can be changed only from the next higher logical level (e.g., the nine-dot problem, or the commonsense mistakes illustrated in the depression, insomnia, and jealousy examples) or, conversely, by attempting second-order change when a first-order change would be appropriate (e.g., when people demand changes of "attitude" and are not content with changes of behavior); *action is taken at the wrong level.*

So fundamentally important, in our experience, are these three ways of mishandling change that they will be dealt with separately in the next three chapters.

4
THE TERRIBLE SIMPLIFICATIONS

My aim is to teach you to pass from a piece of disguised nonsense to something that is patent nonsense.

—WITTGENSTEIN

THAT anybody should attempt to deal with difficult situations by denying that a problem is a problem appears, at first sight, rather unlikely. However, even colloquial language reflects this in expressions such as "putting one's head into the sand," "whistling past the graveyard," "if you don't look it will go away," and the like. In more abstract terms, the typical formula involved here is: there is no problem (or, at worst, it's merely a difficulty) and anybody who sees a problem must be mad or bad—in fact, he may be the only source of whatever difficulty is admitted. That is, denial of problems and attacks on those either pointing them out or trying to deal with them go together. Since we believe that circular, not linear and unidirectional, causality is involved in human interaction (at any of various levels—a family, a business organization, a political system, and so on), there is no need to get embroiled in chicken-or-egg questions about what comes first here or in any of the examples to follow.

This compound of denial and attack depends upon gross simplification of the complexities of interaction in social systems and, more generally, of our modern, highly complex, interdependent, and quickly changing world. This stance can be maintained only by refusing to see this complexity, and then defining one's tunnel vision as a realistic and honest attitude towards life, or as "hard-headed sticking to the facts." The French term *terribles simplificateurs*, born after the events of May 1968, seems especially apt for the exponents of this stance.

Nothing that has been said so far should be construed as implying that simplification is always inappropriate, or not conducive to change. In fact, the history of science shows very clearly that in the course of time scientific theories tend to become more and more complex as scientists try to accommodate more and more exceptions and inconsistencies into the overall premises of a theory. It may then take a genius to throw this patchwork out and find a new, elegant set of premises to account for the phenomena under study.[1] But this kind of simplification is then precisely a second-order change. And needless to say, there are geniuses and "geniuses." The ingeniousness of many a so-called genius may be nothing but the inability to grasp the complexity of a situation, or a callous disregard for the rights of others. In this latter perspective, the violation of inconvenient rules or other forms of gangster-like behavior may indeed appear the courage of a genius.

The function of denial as a defense mechanism plays an important role in psychoanalytic theory, but it is generally limited there to unconscious needs and drives which are prevented from rising into consciousness through the denial of their existence. By contrast, our work has taught us that the interpersonal effects of denying undeniable problems (which may themselves be quite conscious) are usually both more serious and more flamboyant than those which in a monadic view could be attributed to the mechanism of denial as an intrapsychic defense.

---

[1]See Kuhn: As we have already seen, normal science ultimately leads only to the recognition of anomalies and to crises. And these are terminated, not by deliberation and interpretation, but by a relatively sudden and unstructured event like the gestalt switch. Scientists then often speak of the "scales falling from the eyes" or of the "lightning flash" that "inundates" a previously obscure puzzle, enabling its components to be seen in a new way that for the first time permits its solution (62).

There can be no doubt that a large part of the process of socialization in any society consists in teaching the young that which they must *not* see, *not* hear, *not* think, feel, or say. Without very definite rules about what should remain outside one's awareness, an orderly society would be as unthinkable as one that fails to teach its members what they must be aware of and communicate about.[2] But as always there are limits and there is an opposite extreme which is reached when the reality distortion inherent in avoidance or denial begins to outweigh its advantages. Lasègue and Falret's *Folie à deux* study (70), written almost one hundred years ago, Lidz's work on the *transmission of irrationality* (73), Wynne's concept of pseudo-mutuality (110), Laing's *collusion* (64) and mystification (66), Scheflen's *gruesome twosome* (83), Ferreira's *family myths* (33)—all these studies are based on the observation of particular aspects of problem denial in disturbed families. First and foremost among the reasons for the denial of problems is probably the need to maintain an acceptable social façade. Among its immediate results are the so-called open secrets in these families. They are open in the sense that everybody knows about them and are secrets in that nobody is supposed to know that everybody else knows. As already mentioned, the

---

[2]This fact, namely that a large part of human communication takes place tacitly, through the absence of communication, is increasingly overlooked by those *terribles simplificateurs* who have jumped on the bandwagon of communications theory and practice, and are basing group and family psychotherapy, marathons, encounter and sensitivity meetings, etc., on the problem-engendering premise that communication should be clear, straightforward, open, direct—in a word, total. But instead of effecting total communication their efforts become at best totalitarian. (For a refreshingly frank and yet thorough treatment of this subject see Kursh's paper "The Benefits of Poor Communication" (63). The absurd simplification inherent in this approach becomes somewhat more evident if we recall that one of the basic laws of information theory is that the occurrence of, say, the letter *a* does not mean "a," it means "not *b* to *z*." Thus even, and especially, at this very fundamental level of information exchange, meaning is actually communicated through that which is not communicated. Or, compare what Lao-tzu has to say on the value of empty space: "Thirty spokes share the wheel's hub; it is the center hole that makes it useful. Shape clay into a vessel; it is the space within that makes it useful. Cut doors and windows for a room; it is the holes which make it useful. Therefore, profit comes from what is there; usefulness from what is not there" (69, Chapter 11).

unconscious element is therefore often quite absent and is replaced by a silent, interpersonal contract, or, as Ferreira puts it: "The individual family member may know, and often does, that much of the [family] image is false and represents no more than a sort of official party line" (32). The expression "party line" is extremely well chosen, for, indeed, party lines serve precisely the same purpose as family myths, though on a much larger scale. Understandably, situations of the kind just described may become much more insidious and pathogenic when not only the existence of a problem is denied, but also the denial itself.[3] These are then the more flamboyant cases of systems pathology, in which even the attempt at pointing at the denial, let alone at the problem itself, is quickly defined as badness or madness, with badness or madness then actually resulting from this type of terrible simplification—unless a person has learned the crucial skill to *see*, but to be judicious in what he *says*. For he who sees behind the facade is damned if he sees and says that he sees, or crazy if he sees but does not even admit it to himself. Or, as Laing (68) has put it:

They are playing a game. They are playing at not playing a game. If I show them I see they are, I shall break the rules and they will punish me. I must play the game, of not seeing that I play the game.

And:

If I don't know I don't know, I think I know;
If I don't know I know, I think I don't know.

Simplifications are equally present in many wider social contexts. We have already pointed out the essential similarity between family myths and party lines. Another area is the pre-election promises of politicians. Their programs are often replete

[3]Esterson has recently published a detailed description of this kind of family interaction (30).

with simplifications, and they rarely fail to sound convincing to large numbers of people. If elected, these men either realize that what they promised is impossible to fulfill, because they find themselves faced with unexpected (but not unexpectable) difficulties, or else they are forced into political brinkmanship. It would certainly be nice if problems simply went away as a result of being denied, or through the use of force. For instance, there can be no doubt that the Electronic Revolution presents society with unheard-of, dehumanizing problems, but it is certain that their solution will not be achieved through some terrible simplification like: Let's smash the computers and go back to the simple, honest life. The upheavals caused by the Industrial Revolution were not solved by the attempted smashing of the machines either, "obvious" as this solution may have appeared at the time.

It is very easy to separate rules from the concrete necessities that lead to their formulation and then to consider it a heroic act to defy this dismembered rule as nothing but an expression of malevolence or prejudice. A middle-aged man with great sympathy for the alienation of young adults told us of a typical disappointment. He had offered two youngsters who were interested in cars free training in his small auto repair shop, an offer which they gladly accepted. But when he told them that in order to protect themselves from serious accidents they would have to tuck in their long hair and wear shoes to work, they could see in this request only the typical prejudice of the older generation with regard to their self-expression.

If this example seems somewhat trivial, consider the same attitude on a larger scale: In a recent study, a team of psychologists at Ohio State University interviewed 102 passengers at Columbus International Airport about airline security measures. Three areas were explored: personal convenience, effectiveness, and their personal preferences for specific measures. One of the findings was that passengers under thirty years of age "are against frisking suspicious-looking passengers, increasing airline fares, im-

prisoning convicted highjackers for life, and combat training for
airline personnel. The fact that younger passengers are against
these four items may possibly be interpreted as representative of
a more general attitude prevalent among contemporary youths"
(25). Unfortunately, the design of this study did not include the
question as to what alternative measures these passengers would
recommend in order to deal with the worldwide problem of air
piracy; that their "more general attitude" may be based on the
typical simplification that this problem is no problem remains,
therefore, an assumption—albeit a fairly plausible one.

This leads to another example of a simplification, namely the
widespread problem encountered by most North American and
European universities in relation to the relevance of modern academic education. Here too we find a sweeping denial of the deep
problems with which the most enlightened thinkers and teachers
have tried to come to terms through the ages. Eulau, in a speech
before the Midwest Political Science Association, has summarized this state of affairs. For him, the rush to relevance (with a
capital R) as an allegedly legitimate demand and a panacea for
the difficulties of acquiring an academic education breeds its own
destruction. Relevance, he points out, is supposed to mean first

[a] simple and immediately comprehensible explanation of what are
really very complicated problems. More often than not, the explanation
is of the one-factor variety; environmental problems are due to the greed
for profits; prison problems are due to the guards' brutality; war is due
to economic imperialism; and so on. Because these matters are urgent,
they require immediate solutions; immediate solutions do not permit
complicated analysis; complicated analysis is only a pretense for doing
nothing.

Second, Relevance means that the content of teaching and research
should be as fresh and up-to-date as the morning news broadcast. Treating events historically or philosophically is a cop-out. Living with the
puzzles created by new events is, however, intolerable. . . . Fourth,
Relevance means committing oneself and all others, whether they are

willing or not, in social and political action. . . . Fifth, Relevance means, at the extreme, that only those who agree with one and are committed to one's own causes should be heard . . . (31).

Many analogous examples of problem-engendering simplifications can be found in the medical field, especially because there emotional factors play a particularly powerful role. The complexity of a disease group like cancer is such that even an accomplished expert can apply himself only to a sub-area of the whole field. Yet, as the controversies over drugs like Krebiozin or Laetrile have shown, it can happen almost overnight that a scientifically worthless compound gets the reputation of the simple and ultimate cure-all. When the experts then deny this, they are sooner or later suspected of wanting to suppress the drug for sinister reasons of their own.

To recapitulate the themes of this chapter: One way of mishandling a problem is to behave as if it did not exist. For this form of denial, we have borrowed the term *terrible simplification*. Two consequences follow from it: a) acknowledgment, let alone any attempted solution, of the problem is seen as a manifestation of madness or badness; and b) the problem requiring change becomes greatly compounded by the "problems" created through its mishandling.

Looking at this impasse in terms of Group Theory, a simplification satisfies the concept of the identity member (the third group property) in that its introduction into an existing problem (itself conceived as a group member) maintains the latter's identity, i.e., leaves the problem unchanged. But since our group members are human problems, which—unlike the abstract and stable group members in mathematics, logic, theoretical physics, etc.—have a tendency to become more intense the longer they remain unsolved (while still maintaining the group's structure), a simplification may turn truly terrible by compounding the original problem.

5
THE UTOPIA SYNDROME

*I have ascertained by full enquiry, that Utopia lies outside the
bounds of the known world.*

—GUILLAUME BUDE

*While we pursue the unattainable we make impossible the real-
izable.*

—ROBERT ARDREY

I F a *terrible simplificateur* is someone who sees no problem where there is one, his philosophical antipode is the utopian
who sees a solution where there is none.[1]

Ours is an age of utopia. Grandiose, esoteric endeavors are not
just a fad, they are a sign of our times. All sorts of *gurus* offer to
rush in where angels fear to tread: "The natural state of man is
ecstatic wonder; we should not settle for less," states the preamble
to the constitution of a Free University. A program offers "a
system of human development carefully structured to produce
lucid thought, emotional balance, and physical joy and serenity.
The result is the total integration of mind, emotion, and body
which is man's true natural condition." Another prospectus introduces a course for married couples with the words: "Marriage
which means the compromise of love isn't worth the trip." And

---

[1]Of course, opposites are more similar than the mid-position they exclude. In fact, the
simplifiers could be seen as claiming that certain utopias already exist. We might even say
that both the simplifier and the utopian strive for a problemless world—the one by denying
that certain difficulties exist at all, the other by acknowledging their existence but defining
them as basically abnormal and therefore capable of resolution. Thus, if we attempt to
keep simplifications and utopias strictly apart, it is for systematic reasons and not because
we are unaware of their practical affinity.

the description of a course offered by a highly respectable institution of higher learning confidently promises: "If your perception of yourself is vague and ephemeral, if you feel your relations with others are awkward and mixed-up, this series of lecture-work-seminars may well turn you on to life and its deep richness and meaning for you." But what if somebody fails to reach his natural state of ecstatic wonder, and what if life's deep richness does not unfold itself?

Since 1516, when Thomas More described that distant island which he gave the name of Utopia ("nowhere"), volumes have been written on the subject of an ideal life. Much less has been said, however, about the concrete individual and societal results of utopian expectations. In our own age, these results as well as their peculiar pathologies are beginning to become evident. Virulent, and no longer limited to particular societal or political systems, they prove that utopian attempts at change lead to very specific consequences, and that these consequences tend to perpetuate or even worsen what was to be changed.

Extremism in the solving of human problems seems to occur most frequently as a result of the belief that one has found (or even *can* find) the ultimate, all-embracing solution. Once somebody holds this belief, it is then logical for him to try to actualize this solution—in fact, he would not be true to his own self if he did not. The resulting behavior, which we shall call the *utopia syndrome*, can take one of three possible forms.

The *first* could be called "introjective." Its consequences are more immediately definable as psychiatric than social, since they are the outcome of a deep, painful feeling of personal inadequacy for being unable to reach one's goal. If that goal is utopian, then the very act of setting it creates a situation in which the unattainability of the goal is not likely to be blamed on its utopian nature but rather on one's ineptitude: my life should be rich and rewarding, but I am living in banality and boredom; I should have intense feelings but cannot awaken them in myself. "Dropping out," depression, withdrawal, or perhaps suicide[2] are likely consequences of this predicament. The program description of a panel discussion on "RAP-Centers" (i.e., Real Alternative Programs—counseling centers where young people can "rap") at the 1971 meeting of the American Ortho-Psychiatric Association summarizes his problem only too well:

These centers' populations differ from those of classic clinic populations in certain ways, e.g., "loneliness" is experienced as "unbearable" and is chronic; fear of "establishment institutions" or of being considered a "patient" precludes treatment elsewhere; expectation of constant instant happiness is not met and its absence is seen by rap-clients as "sickness"; inherent, indoctrinated concern with police (even when not warranted) is endemic; training in order to "help" is considered unnecessary and even harmful. Yet more people go to RAP-Centers than to Community Mental Health Clinics (54).

Other possible consequences of this form of the utopia syndrome are alienation, divorce, nihilistic world views; frequently alcohol or drugs are involved, and their brief euphorias are inevitably followed by a return to an even colder, grayer reality, a return which makes existential "dropping out" even more appealing.

The second variation of the utopia syndrome is much less dramatic and may even hold a certain charm. Its motto is Robert Louis Stevenson's well-known aphorism, "It is better to travel hopefully than to arrive," which he probably borrowed from a Japanese proverb. Rather than condemning oneself for being unable to effect a utopian change, one indulges in a relatively

[2]See Yalom and Yalom's paper on Hemingway: "When the idealized image is severe and unattainable, as it was for Hemingway, tragic consequences may result: the individual cannot in real life approximate the superhuman scope of the idealized image, reality eventually intrudes, and he realizes the discrepancy between what he wants to be and what he is in actuality. At this point he is flooded with self-hatred, which is expressed through a myriad of self-destructive mechanisms from subtle forms of self-torment (the tiny voice which whispers, Christ, you're ugly! when one gazes into a mirror) to total annihilation of the self" (111).

harmless and almost playful form of procrastination. Since the goal is distant, the journey will be long, and a long journey requires lengthy preparations. The uneasy question as to whether the goal can be reached at all, or, if reached, will be worth the long trip, need not be asked for the time being. In his poem *Ithaka,* the Greek poet Constantinos Cavafy depicts this very attitude. Pray that the way be long, he counsels the seafarer, that your journey be full of adventures and experiences. You must always have Ithaka in mind, arrival there is your predestination—but do not hurry the journey, better that it last many years. Be quite old when you anchor at the island. And Cavafy knows of a non-utopian solution: You enter harbors never seen before, and rich with all you have gained on the way, do not expect Ithaka to give you riches. Ithaka has given you your lovely journey, without Ithaka you would not have set out. But Cavafy's wise, conciliatory solution is open only to a few, for the dream of arriving in utopia can be alarming: either as fear of disenchantment or, in Hamlet's sense, that we would "rather bear those ills we have than fly to others that we know not of." In either case, it is the journey, not the arrival, that matters; the eternal student, the perfectionist, the person who repeatedly manages to fail on the eve of success are examples of travelers who eternally wander and never arrive. The psychology of the unattainable necessitates that every actual fulfillment is experienced as a loss, as a profanation: for the devout Jew the political reality of the State of Israel is little more than the banal parody of an age-old, messianic longing; for the romantic lover who at long last conquers the beautiful woman, the reality of his victory is a far cry from what it was in his dreams. George Bernard Shaw put the same thought even more succinctly and pessimistically: "There are two tragedies in life. One is not to get your heart's desire. The other is to get it."

This form of utopianism becomes problematic in everyday life when a person seriously expects that "arriving"—as opposed to a view of life as an ongoing process—will be completely nonproblematic. It is of interest to us that, for example, many major transitions in life are described in the popular mythology as trouble-free, totally delightful experiences: the newlyweds cheered on by friends and relatives (and, of course, by furniture stores): "we know you will have a happy life together"; the "magic" of the honeymoon; the young couple, about to have their first child, who are met with statements about the joys of parenthood and how much closer this will bring them; retirement as both a state of serene fulfillment and the opening up of new possibilities; the enchantment of (literally) arriving in that distant, exotic city, etc., etc. Yet, as is well known, all these transitions normally involve some personal discomfort, difficulty, and disappointment.

The *third* variation of the utopia syndrome is essentially "projective"; its basic ingredient is a moral, righteous stance based on the conviction of having found the truth and sustained by the resulting missionary responsibility of changing the world. This is first attempted by various forms of persuasion and in the hope that the truth, if only made plain enough, will of necessity be seen by all men of good will. Consequently, those who will not embrace it, or will not even listen to it, must be acting in bad faith, and their destruction for the benefit of mankind may eventually appear justified.[3] Thus, if my life is not in a permanent state of ecstatic wonder, if universal love of everybody for everybody has not yet been actualized, if in spite of my exercises I have not yet attained *sátori*, if I am still unable to communicate deeply and meaningfully with my partner, if sex remains a disappointingly mediocre experience, a far cry from what the numerous sex manuals describe—then this is because my parents, or society at large, by their rules and limitations, have crippled me and are unwilling to concede me that simple freedom needed for my self-actualiza-

---

[3] These premises are, of course, also terribly simplistic, but there is an essential difference between "simplifiers" and "utopians." With the former, a problem is denied; with the latter a difficulty is seen, indeed proclaimed and fervently attacked, but in a totally counterproductive way.

tion. "Wir vom System krankgemachte Typen" (we, whom the Establishment has made sick): this is how some German radicals describe themselves. But this is also Rousseau revisited: "Que la nature a fait l'homme heureux et bon, mais que la société le déprave et le rend misérable." Robert Ardrey, quoting this opening sentence of *Émile*, believes that it launched what he so aptly calls the Age of Alibi: nature made me happy and good, and if I am otherwise, it is society's fault. The Age of Alibi, Ardrey writes in *The Social Contract,*

presenting greater sympathy for the violator than the violated, has with elegance prepared us for maximum damage as we face a future of maximum civil disorder. A philosophy which for decades has induced us to believe that human fault must rest always on somebody else's shoulders; that responsibility for behavior damaging to society must invariably be attributed to society itself; that human beings are born not only perfectible but identical, so that any unpleasant divergences must be the product of unpleasant environments; . . . such a philosophy has prepared in all splendour the righteous self-justifications of violent minorities, and has likewise prepared with delicate hands the guilts and the bewilderments of the violated (8).

Within his own framework, Alfred Adler already was quite aware of similar projective mechanisms, e.g., when defining his concept of an individual's life plan. "The life plan of the neurotic demands categorically that if he fails, it should be through someone else's fault and that he should be freed from personal responsibility" (1). And concerning paranoia, Adler writes: "The activity [of the paranoiac] is usually of a very belligerent kind. The patient blames others for the lack of success in his exaggerated plans, and his active striving for complete superiority results in an attitude of hostility towards others. . . . His hallucinations . . . arise always when the patient wants something unconditionally, yet at the same time wants to be considered free from responsibility" (2).

Since in spite, or perhaps just because, of their utopian nature, such proposed solutions are astonishingly pedestrian and inadequate—in Ardrey's words, the clichés of a century, all tried and found wanting (6)—the belief in their uniqueness and pristine originality can be maintained only by a studious disregard for the evidence of the past. A deliberate disdain not only for the lessons of history, but for the whole idea that history has anything to offer, becomes another essential ingredient of the utopia syndrome. This has the additional advantage of enabling one to see one's own suffering and the sorry state of the world as a unique, unheard-of plight for which there are no valid comparisons. Those who ignore history, warned Santayana, are doomed to repeat it.

We have so far considered cases of self- or world-improvement in the service of an unrealistic ideal in which the attempted change compounds some unchangeable difficulty into a problem. But it also can happen that people will consider the *absence* of a difficulty to be a problem that requires corrective action, and act until they have a full-grown pseudo-problem on their hands. A fruitful matrix for such "problems" is, for instance, puritanism (whose basic rule has been facetiously defined as: You may do anything as long as you don't enjoy it). The premise here is that life is hard, that it requires constant sacrifice, and that all success has to be paid for dearly. Within the frame of this premise, the occurrence of ease, spontaneity, and "undeserved" pleasure, let along of any sort of windfall, is seen as signifying the existence of something wrong or a portent of imminent vengeance of the gods.[4] The woman who upholds motherhood as a glorious sacrifice comes to mind ("Oh yes, I had morning sickness—I enjoyed every bit of it" [91]), or the compulsive husband who lives only for his work—although in their view the problem is usually the

---

[4]One is reminded of Till Eulenspiegel, who, trudging through the rolling countryside of the Ardennes, cried while walking downhill but laughed while climbing the steep crests. When asked for the reason for this strange behavior, he explained that while going downhill he was thinking of the rise awaiting him on the other side of the valley, but during the climbs he was already anticipating the pleasure of the easy descent.

"irresponsible" behavior of a child or of the spouse. Another example is the bright student who takes all academic hurdles with ease, but increasingly worries about the moment of truth, the final denouement, when it will be obvious that he really knows nothing and has so far only been "lucky." Or then there are the "D-Day specialists"—people who constantly train themselves to be ready for some weird emergency, the occurrence of which is only a matter of time and will require all their physical prowess and survival know-how. In all these cases, the premise involves a negative utopia: the better things are, the worse they really are—so they must be made more difficult. Positive utopias imply "no problems," negative ones "no solutions"; both of them define the normal difficulties and pleasures of life as abnormalities.

Common to all aspects of the utopia syndrome is the fact that the premises on which the syndrome is based are considered to be more real than reality. What we mean by this is that the individual (or, for that matter, a group or a whole society), when trying to order his world in accordance with his premise and seeing his attempt fail, will typically not examine the premise for any absurd or unrealistic elements of its own, but will, as we have seen, blame outside factors (e.g., society) or his own ineptitude. The idea that the fault might lie with the premises is unbearable, for the premises are the truth, are reality. Thus, the Maoists argue, if after more than half a century the Soviet brand of Marxism has not managed to create the ideal, classless society, it is because the pure doctrine has fallen into impure hands, and not because there might be something inherently wrong with Marxism. The same stance is familiar in unproductive research projects, when the attempted solution is *more* money, a *bigger* project—in short, "more of the same."

This distinction between facts and premises about the facts is crucial for an understanding of the vicissitudes of change. We have already referred to it when presenting the nine-dot problem, where—it will be remembered—it is a fallacious assumption about the problem which precludes its solution, and not the fact that one has not yet discovered the "right" way of connecting the dots within the frame of that premise. That this mistake is far from trivial becomes clearer when we examine it in the potentially fatal context of existential despair. Many people are led to contemplate, or even commit, suicide because, like Hemingway, they are unable to live up to certain expectations. This is why they may begin to experience their lives as meaningless; existential writers, from Kierkegaard and Dostoyevsky to Camus, have dealt with the lethal consequences of the lack of meaning. In this form of existential despair the search for a meaning in life is central and all-pervasive, so much so that the seeker may question everything under the sun, *except* his quest itself, that is, the unquestioned assumption that there *is* a meaning and that he has to discover it in order to survive.[5] Flippant as it may sound, this is the difference between much of human tragedy and the attitude of the King of Hearts in *Alice in Wonderland*, who, after reading the nonsensical poem of the White Rabbit, cheerfully concludes: "If there is no meaning in it, that saves a world of trouble, you know, as we needn't try to find any."

But we are again getting ahead of ourselves by mentioning solutions while we are still on the subject of problem formation. This is almost inevitable, for, as we have seen, a "solution" may itself be the problem. And it is especially so in those areas which are specifically concerned with change, i.e., in psychotherapy and in the wider field of social, economic, and political changes.

As for psychotherapy and utopianism, the question arises if and to what extent treatment may itself suffer from the affliction it is supposed to cure. With the possible exception of the writings

---

[5]Or cf. Laing: "Illusionment or disillusionment may equally be based on the same fantasy. There is 'an answer' somewhere; or there is 'no answer' anywhere. The same issue either way" (65).

of Alfred Adler, Harry Stack Sullivan, and Karen Horney, most schools of psychotherapy (although not necessarily their individual adherents) have set themselves utopian goals, e.g., genital organization, individuation, self-actualization—to say nothing of the more modern and extreme schools mentioned at the beginning of this chapter. With goals such as these, psychotherapy becomes an open-ended process, perhaps humanistic, but more likely inhumane as far as the concrete suffering of patients goes. In view of the lofty magnitude of the endeavor, it would be unreasonable to expect concrete, rapid change, and in a fascinating, almost Orwellian display of logical acrobatics, the concrete is thus labeled utopian, and utopia defined as a practical possibility. Make concrete change of a concrete problem dependent upon the reaching of a goal which is so distant as to border infinity, and the resulting situation becomes self-sealing, to borrow Lipson's (74) term. For instance, if an acute case of appendicitis is not cured by the power of the patient's prayer, this merely proves that his faith was not strong enough and his demise "therefore" confirms rather than invalidates the doctrine of spiritual healing. Or, to take a less blatant example, if a "neurotic" symptom is merely seen as that tip of the iceberg, and if in spite of many months of uncovering therapy it has not improved, this "proves" the correctness of the assumption that emotional problems may have their roots in the deepest layers of the unconscious, which in turn explains why the patient needs further and even deeper analysis. Open-ended, self-sealing doctrines win either way, as in the bitter joke about the patient who after years of treatment still wets his bed, "but now I understand why I do it."

Utopian attempts at change create impasses in which it often becomes impossible to distinguish clearly between problems and "problems," and between "problems" and "solutions." The unattainability of a utopia is a pseudo-problem, but the suffering it entails is very real. "If men define situations as real, they are real in their consequence," remarked Thomas (90). If, in a logical *salto mortale*, these consequences are seen as the causes of the problem, it then makes sense to try and change them. If these attempts are unsuccessful (as they have to be), it then makes sense to try more of the same. "The difficult we do right away, the impossible takes a little longer"—a clever aphorism, but a cruel trap for anyone who even half believes in it. The impossible, obviously, takes forever, but in the meantime, to quote Ardrey once more, "while we pursue the unattainable we make impossible the realizable" (5). We smile at the joke about the drunk who is searching for his keys not where he really lost them, but under the street lamp, because that's where the light is best. It sounds funny, but only because the joke makes it explicit that a solution is attempted not only away from the problem (and is therefore doomed to fail), but also because the fruitless search could go on forever—again, the attempted solution *is* the problem. In everyday life situations, this fact usually remains outside the awareness of all concerned; the cure is not simply worse than the disease, but rather *is* the disease. For example: Quite obviously, few—if any—marriages live up to the ideals contained in some of the classic marriage manuals or popular mythology. Those who accept these ideas about what a marital relationship should "really" be are likely to see their marriage as problematic and to start working towards its solution until divorce do them part. Their concrete problem is not their marriage, but their attempts at finding the solution to a problem which in the first place is not a problem, and which, even if it were one, could not be solved on the level on which they attempt to change it.

From the foregoing, one arrives at the disturbing possibility that the limits of a responsible and humane psychotherapy may be much narrower than is generally thought. Lest therapy become its own pathology, it must limit itself to the relief of suffering; the quest for happiness cannot be its task. From aspirin we expect a lessening of our headache, but not also ingenious thoughts, nor even the prevention of future headaches. This, basically, is also true of therapy. When an eager pupil, in his frantic quest for *sátori,* asked the Zen master what enlightenment was like, he answered: "Coming home and resting comfortably."

On the socioeconomic and political levels, the situation can be viewed as similar, except that there the sobering conclusions to be drawn may appear, if anything, even more shocking and backward. A recent article in a leading Swiss daily summarizes the international monetary situation in terms which sound surprisingly familiar: "We now recognize that for years we have been confusing cause and effects in monetary matters. . . . Without imposing a limitation on our futuristic expectations and their mythical implications, all attempts at fighting inflation are doomed to failure. It can even be said that modern expansionistic policies indirectly create the ills which they are supposed to combat" (24). Similarly, the sophisticated and highly developed social welfare programs of Sweden, Denmark, Britain, Austria, and other countries have reached a point where these programs are *creating* new needs and thereby defeating their own purposes. In the United States, the situation is not much different. In a lecture on what he pointedly calls "The Functions of Incompetence," Thayer recently noted the astonishing fact that between 1968 and 1970—that is, in just two years—social welfare expenditures increased about 34 percent from $11 billion to $14 billion. This proves not only that these welfare measures are needed, but something else: that thousands of specialized jobs are also needed for the implementation of these programs, "and that the continued growth of this part of our total economy will depend upon increasing—not decreasing—the incompetence of the citizenry in all of those dimensions for which there is a welfare program, or for which a program might be invented and funded" (89).

But increased incompetence is not the only problem we are facing. As early as 1947, in his essay "Utopia and Violence," the philosopher Karl Popper warned that utopian schemes must perforce lead to new crises. It is unfortunately much easier, he points out, to propose ideal and abstract goals and to find enthusiastic followers than to solve *concrete* problems. But, warns Popper, "our fellow men have a claim to our help. No generation must be sacrificed for the sake of future generations, for the sake of an ideal of happiness that may never be realized. In brief, it is my thesis that human misery is the most urgent problem of a rational public policy and that happiness is not such a problem. The attainment of happiness should be left to our private endeavours" (78). And long before Popper, the poet Hölderlin remarked: "What has made the State into hell is that man wanted to make it his heaven."

It would be difficult to define the utopia syndrome more succinctly. But let us go one step further and consider what would happen if utopian change were ever achieved, for instance on the sociopolitical level. It would, first of all, presuppose that the ideal society would be composed of individuals who in their ideal and equal degree of maturity would all be thinking, feeling, and acting alike—a fallacy which conjures up the night-marish image of totally sterile, stagnant masses or of von Neumannian robots, deprived of that vital tension which comes only from the natural diversity of men. And this is the even more frightening aspect: that change, and with it any stirring of individuality and creativity, would have to be outlawed, for it could only be a return from perfection to imperfection. This, then, would be an Orwellian society in which those who in our days clamor loudest for utopian change would be the first to disappear behind barbed wire or the walls of asylums. The vicious circle would be definitively closed and the ideal solution would have become the Final Solution.

The utopia syndrome is a pathology that goes beyond what the more orthodox theories of symptom formation have taught us. If we see in its manifestations merely the results of intrapsychic conflict due to the pressures of an excessively rigid superego (as psychodynamic theory would suggest), or of a neurotically ambitious life plan (as an Adlerian might interpret most of the examples cited), we lose sight of what is crucial: that a certain way of mishandling change, attempted for *whatever* internal or external, "conscious" or "unconscious" reasons, has consequences *all of its own* that cannot be reduced to the status of mere epiphenomena without making the reduction itself part of the pathology. The utopia syndrome is an example of what the biologist would call an *emergent quality*—something more than and different from the sum of the ingredients that go into its making. It is a *Gestalt* in the classic sense of gestalt psychology (Wertheimer, Koffka, Bühler, etc.), a *structure* in the sense of modern structuralism.

As every high school student knows, the introduction of zero or infinity into an equation produces paradoxical results. In the preceding chapter, we examined the consequences of introducing zero. In this chapter, we have examined a way of attempting second-order change which may be called the introduction of infinity. To the best of our knowledge, this possibility is not envisaged by Group Theory, although it could be argued that if the combination rule of a given group is division by infinity, the outcome is the identity member. In this sense the introduction of infinity would be a special case of group property *d*. We are not competent to argue this point, especially since our references to Group Theory are clearly intended to be in the nature of a thought model and not of mathematical proof. But where we believe we are on theoretically safe ground is this: At the root of the protean manifestations of the utopia syndrome there lies a discrepancy between actuality and potentiality, that is, between the way things *are* and the way they *should be* according to a certain premise. This discrepancy calls for change which, at least theoretically, could be applied to either actuality or potentiality in order to close the painful gap between them. Practically there exist many situations in which reality can be changed to conform to a premise. But there are probably as many situations in which nothing can be done about the actual state of things. If in any one of these situations the postulated potentiality (the "should be" state) is considered more real than reality, then change will be attempted where it cannot be achieved *and* where it would not even have to be attempted if the utopian premise were not postulated in the first place. Thus, it is the premise that things *should be* a certain way which is the problem and which requires change, and not the way things *are*. Without the utopian premise, the actuality of the situation might be quite bearable. So what is involved here is a mishandling of change: first-order change is attempted where only second-order change can lead to a solution.

6
PARADOXES

All Cretans are liars.

—EPIMENIDES OF CRETE, Sixth century B.C.

I THINK what I am trying to say is: I want Andy to learn to do things, and I want him to do things—but I want *him* to want to do them. I mean, he could follow orders blindly and not want to. I realize that I am making a mistake, I cannot pinpoint what I am doing wrong, but I cannot agree with dictating to him what to do—yet, if a child were to be put completely on his own like that, he would eventually be mired down into a room this deep [referring to clothes, toys, etc., on the floor] or whatever—no, these are—there are two extremes. I want him to *want* to do things, but I realize it's going to be something that we have to *teach* him.

These are the words of a mother explaining her difficulties as she tries to change the behavior of her eight-year-old, who does not like to do his homework. Even if she knew that she has caught herself and him in a paradox, this knowledge would hardly lessen her bewilderment, for the baffling nature of paradox has occupied greater minds for many centuries.

It is usually asserted that if paradox appears to create an untenable situation, the impasse can be resolved by recourse to the fact that such a situation is a logical impossibility and, therefore, of no practical importance. Thus, the village barber who is to shave all and only those men in the village who do not shave themselves, or the mailman who is to deliver the mail to all and only those people who do not pick it up themselves at the post office, are not "really" in a predicament as far as their own beards or their own letters are concerned, because as long as we remain strictly within the field of formal logic there cannot, by definition, be such a barber, mailman, or village. From a logical point of view this may be unquestionable, but since we have all experienced "illogical" behavior and situations in our daily lives, this all too logical view leaves us dissatisfied.

To the best of our knowledge, it was Wittgenstein who first speculated on the practical, behavioral implications of paradox: "The various half-joking guises of logical paradox are only of interest in so far as they remind anyone of the fact that a serious form of the paradox is indispensable if we are to understand its function properly. The question arises: what part can such a logical mistake play in a language game?" Wittgenstein then makes reference to the paradox of the king (who had promulgated a law according to which every arriving foreigner had to state the true reason for his entry into the kingdom; those who did not tell the truth were to be hanged, which prompted a sophist to state that his reason for coming was to get hanged on the strength of this law) and asks the crucial question: "What kind of rules must the king give to escape henceforth from the awkward position which his prisoner has put him in?—What sort of a problem is this?" (105).

The first systematic study of the behavioral effects of paradox in human communication was carried out by a research group headed by the anthropologist Gregory Bateson. This work led to the postulation of the Double-Bind Theory of schizophrenia (16). Subsequent work, however, suggests that schizophrenia is only a special case to which this theory obtains and that, depending on the basic parameters of a given human situation, it is generally applicable to other types of disturbed communication, including non-psychotic patterns of human interaction; in fact, the inadvertent creation of paradox is yet a third, very typical way in which difficulties or needed change can be mishandled. Since we have dealt with the nature and the effect of paradox elsewhere in greater detail (94), let us merely mention here two more recent, outstanding studies in this field, namely the work of the British psychiatrist Ronald D. Laing—especially his brilliant and exasperating book *Knots* (68)—and the findings of an Argentine research team headed by the psychiatrist Carlos E. Sluzki and the sociologist Eliseo Verón (85).

Briefly, what is meant by the behavioral effects of paradox in human communication is the peculiar impasse which arises when messages structured precisely like the classic paradoxes in formal logic are exchanged. A good example of such a message is "Be spontaneous!" (or any one of its possible variations; cf. for example, the cartoon below)—i.e., the demand for behavior which by its very nature can only be spontaneous, but cannot be spontaneous as a result of having been requested. This is precisely the dilemma created by the well-meaning mother mentioned above. She wants her child to comply with what she demands of him, not because she demands it, but spontaneously, of his own will. For instance, instead of the simple demand, "I want you to study" (which the child can either obey or disobey), she demands, "I want you to *want* to study." This requires that the child not only do the right thing (i.e., study), but do the right thing for the right reason (i.e., study because he *wants* to), which a) makes it punishable to do the right thing for the wrong reason (i.e., study because he has been told to and might otherwise be punished), and b) requires that he perform a weird piece of mental acrobatics by making himself want what he does not want and, by implication, also want what is being done to him. For the mother, too, the situation is now untenable. The way she attempts to change her child's behavior makes impossible what she wants to achieve, and she is just as caught as he. Of course, she could force him to study, and apply more of the same force if he still refuses to, which could lead to an appropriate and satisfactory first-order change in terms of group property *d* (i.e., through the introduction of the recipro-

Figure 4. *I was a fool to marry you—I thought I could train you to become a real man!*

cal member).[1] But this is not what she wants. She wants spontaneous compliance, not just obedience to a rule. A similar situation, frequently encountered in marital conflicts, is created by the spouse who wishes certain behaviors from the other, "but only if she/he really wants to—if I have to tell her/him, it's no good."

What sort of a problem is this? we may ask with Wittgenstein. If it is true that all Cretans are liars,[2] then Epimenides spoke the truth, but then the truth is that he is lying. He is therefore truthful when he lies and lying when he is truthful. Paradox arises through the self-reflexiveness of the statement, that is, through a confusion of member and class. Epimenides' statement refers to all his statements and therefore also to this statement itself, since the latter is merely one member of the class of all his statements. A slightly amplified but structurally identical version of his famous dictum may make this a little more obvious: "Whatever I say is a lie [this refers to all his statements and consequently to the class], therefore, I am also lying when I say, 'I am lying' [this refers to this one statement and consequently to a member of the class]."

The structure of every "Be spontaneous!" paradox—and therefore also the mother's request, "I want you to want to study"— is analogous. It imposes the rule that behavior should not be rule-compliant, but spontaneous.[3] This rule therefore says that

---

[1]This, then, is an example of an attempted second-order change where a first-order change is appropriate, as mentioned briefly at the end of Chapter 3. That is, a change in "attitude" is demanded and a "mere" change of behavior is not considered good enough.

[2]The statement is known to us only indirectly through a reference in Paul's letter to Titus (1: 10–12): "There are many irresponsible teachers . . . who are empty talkers and deceivers. These must be silenced. They are upsetting whole families by teaching things they have no right to teach—and all for sordid gain! A man of Crete, one of their own prophets, has testified, *'Cretans have ever been liars, beasts, and lazy gluttons,'* and this is the simple truth." While Paul does not name Epimenides, Clement of Alexandria says that Epimenides of Crete is the man "who is mentioned by the Apostle Paul in his letter to Titus."

[3]*Spontaneous:* arising without external constraint or stimulus; controlled and directed internally; developing without apparent external influence, force, cause, or treatment (Webster's).

compliance with an external rule is unacceptable behavior, since this same behavior should be freely motivated from within. But this basic rule, involving (the class of) all rules, is itself a rule, it is a member of the class and applies to itself. Epimenides as well as the mother thus violate the central axiom of the Theory of Logical Types, i.e., that whatever involves all of a collection (class) cannot be one of the collection (a member).[4] The result is paradox.

We are now in a better position to appreciate the particular form of problem formation inherent in some of the introductory examples cited in Chapter 3. The insomniac typically places himself in a "Be spontaneous!" paradox; he tries to achieve a natural, spontaneous phenomenon, sleep, by an act of will power, and he stays awake. Similarly, the depressed person attempts to change his mood by concentrating on the feelings that he should have to "bring himself out of his depression"—and "should" implies, of course, that feelings can somehow be programmed to arise spontaneously, if one only tries honestly enough.

"Be spontaneous!" paradoxes also figure prominently in the

---

[4]By way of illustration, we have already cited Groucho Marx's refusal to join a club that would be prepared to accept somebody like him as a member. Another example would be this: Imagine that around December 10 somebody buys a box of Christmas cards and asks the salesgirl to gift-wrap it. A typical paradoxical confusion arises between the content (the cards) and the frame defining the content (the gift-wrapping): if it is a Christmas gift, as the wrapping would define it, then its content is senseless—Christmas cards are to be sent out individually and before Christmas. But if the cards are so used, then the gift-wrapping is senseless. In other words, if this strange package is a Christmas gift, then it is not, and if it is not, then it is.

During one of those rather friendly, occasional encounters that apparently used to take place a long, long time ago between the good Lord and the devil, the latter "proved" to God that He was not almighty by asking Him to create a rock that was so enormously big not even God Himself could jump over it. God's reply has not been handed down to us, but the story appears to have created dismay among the twelfth-century scholastics. It is typified by Hugo of St. Victor's almost touching attempt to salvage God's omnipotence, an attempt which is a good example of the impasse into which the attempted solution of paradoxes can easily lead. For, at the end of his reasoning, Hugo sees no other way of extricating himself from the tangle of his own "proofs" than by flatly negating God's ability to do the impossible, reaching the odd conclusion that to be able to do the impossible is not evidence of omnipotence, but rather of impotence: "Deus impossibilia non potest; impossibilia posse non est posse, sed non posse."

way people attempt to change sexual difficulties. Sexual arousal or an orgasm are spontaneous phenomena; the more strongly they are willed, awaited, and desired, the less likely they are to occur. One fairly safe way of turning a sexual encounter into a failure is to plan and premeditate it in luxurious detail.[5] Clinical experience suggests that many instances of sexual unresponsiveness may be related to the desperate attempts of the female during intercourse to "somehow" produce in herself those sensations which, according to her expectations or some sex manual, she *should* have at any given point during intercourse. It will be noticed that in all these instances there are no utopias involved; after all, falling asleep or having certain feelings or sexual responses are very natural phenomena.

Dictatorships almost inevitably impose similar paradoxes. They are not content with mere compliance with common-sense laws (which by and large is all that is required in a democracy); they want to change people's thoughts, values, and outlooks. Mere compliance or lip service is not only not enough, but is in itself considered a form of passive resistance, and even that particular form of silence which under Hitler was called "inner emigration" becomes a sign of hostility. One may not simply put up with coercion, one must want it. One may not merely sign the fantastic confession and get it over and done with, one must believe this confession and truly repent, as described fictionally in *Darkness at Noon* (58) or *1984* (76), biographically in *The Accused* (100) or *Child of the Revolution* (72), to mention just a few examples, and as actually practiced in brain-washing. But the method does not, cannot lead to the desired result, and at the end of his toil the mind-rapist finds himself with either a corpse, a psychotic, or a robot-like *apparatchik;* and none of these changes is anywhere near what he set out to achieve.

But it would be a mistake to believe that similar paradoxes

---

[5]To quote from yet another esoteric training program, this one entitled "Sensuality for Singles": "Finding mature pleasure in deep relationships results from careful planning. . . ."

cannot arise under a less totalitarian system of government, and in this sense the difference between a repressive and a permissive society is unfortunately only one of degree and not of substance. No society can afford not to defend itself against deviance, not to attempt to change those who oppose its rules and structure. In spite of thousands of volumes on the subject of penology, the philosophy of justice has never been, and perhaps never will be, able to lift the function of punishment out of the paradoxical contamination of retaliation, deterrence, and reform. Of these three functions the last, reform, is unfortunately at the same time the most paradoxical as well as the most humane. While we are clearly not competent to deal with the extremely intricate problems of a humane administration of criminal justice, the impasses produced by the attempted changes of an offender's mind and of his behavior can nevertheless be appreciated also by the layman. Whether the setting is a maximum-security prison or merely Juvenile Hall, the paradox is the same: the degree to which the offender has supposedly been reformed by these institutions is judged on the basis of his saying and doing the "right" things *because he has been reformed,* and not because he has merely learned to speak the "right" language and to go through the "right" motions. Reform, when seen as something different from compliance, inevitably becomes self-reflexive—it is then supposed to be both its own cause and its own effect. This game is won by the good "actors"; the only losers are those inmates who refuse to be reformed because they are too "honest" or too angry to play the game, or those who allow it to be apparent that they are playing the game only because they want to get out, and are therefore not acting spontaneously. Humaneness thus creates its own hypocrises, which leads to the melancholy conclusion that in this specific sense it seems preferable to establish a price to be paid for an offense, i.e., a punishment, but to leave the offender's mind alone and thereby to avoid the troublesome consequences of mind-control paradoxes.

Another social institution ostensibly devoted to change is the mental hospital. Not surprisingly it, too, is plagued with problems arising out of the interpenetration of required compliance and expected spontaneity, except that there the problems may be compounded beyond description by the fact that the hospitalized patient is considered unable to make the right decisions by himself—they have to be made for him and for his own good. If he fails to see this, his failure is yet another proof of his incapacity. This creates a terribly paradoxical situation requiring patients and staff to "play at not playing" the game of getting well. Sanity in the hospital is that conduct which is in keeping with very definite norms; these norms should be obeyed spontaneously and not because they are imposed; as long as they have to be imposed, the patient is considered sick. This being so, the old strategy for obtaining one's speedy release from a mental hospital is more than a joke:

A. develop a flamboyant symptom that has considerable nuisance value for the whole ward;
B. attach yourself to a young doctor in need of his first successes;
C. let him cure you rapidly of your "symptom"; and
D. make him thus into the most fervent advocate of your regained sanity.

So far we have been citing examples from what Goffman (42) calls total institutions. But there are also far less repressive contexts which are in the service of change, and which in the process may get entangled in similar paradoxes precluding the attempted change. Psychoanalysis, for instance, has been facetiously defined as the disease for which it is supposed to be the cure—an aphorism which reflects very well its paradoxical, self-reflexive nature, but which overlooks the curative aspects to which paradox is here applied with or without the analyst's awareness, as Jackson and Haley (52) have shown in their classic paper on transference. But one aspect of psychoanalysis has much more untenable consequences than the doctor-patient relationship: the relationship between a candidate in training and his training analyst. The personal analysis of a future analyst is an important part of his training. In the course of this analysis, he is supposed to come to grips with at least those major neurotic personality trends that might interfere most seriously with his future work. The course and outcome of the training analysis thus becomes one of the most decisive criteria for evaluating whether his diploma should be granted or withheld.[6] This places him in a far more paradoxical position than if he were a patient. He is expected to change, and the degree of his accomplished change is inferred from mental manifestations that are considered among the most spontaneous, namely dreams and free associations. While there is little to prevent a determined patient from simply discontinuing his analysis or switching to another analyst, these exits are not open to the training candidate. On the one hand, he is expected to be completely spontaneous and truthful in his communications with his trainer; on the other hand, he knows that if his spontaneity is not yet of the right kind, his training analyst cannot recommend his graduation. Therefore, in this strange interpersonal context even compliance itself is not good enough; but noncompliance is completely out of the question.

This brings us once again to the general problems inherent in the vast field of education, itself an institution of change par excellence. We have already mentioned the concept of relevance; let us here merely point to a universal variation of the mother's "Be spontaneous!" paradox. It lies hidden in the claim, "School is fun" (or even "School should be fun"), a fiction so dear to the hearts of parents and educators alike, but so remote from the actual experience of students generally. But let us not underestimate the power of such social dogma, especially for a child. No explanation typically accompanies this message, and this, if anything, reinforces rather than invalidates it, the implication being

[6]In this connection cf. (86) and Szasz (87).

that it is self-explanatory. So there is not only "something the matter with me if I do not like school, but also I must be bad or stupid for being unable to see how school is fun, when everybody else apparently can see it so clearly." Another possible reaction is: "I am not being treated the same as other students, that's why it isn't fun."

In the traditional system of education, the teacher was acknowledged as the authority and determined the subject matter to be learned. In modern education, strenuous attempts are being made to democratize his role, but this creates troublesome paradoxes very similar to that of the mother and her little son who did not want to do his homework. Educators can generally be expected to have expertise about the value of various studies, but there is no "democratic" way in which they can demand that the students engage in these studies. Yet, if it were left to the students to decide "democratically" what they wish to study or not, or, for that matter, if they want to come to school or not, the result would be chaos. Thus all the teacher can do is to use subtle methods of influencing the students' minds in the "right" direction, by somehow convincing them (and preferably also himself) that these are "teaching techniques" and not covert means of coercion—since coercion is anathema to the cherished ideal of spontaneity.

Human relations in general are an area in which paradox can arise easily and inadvertently in the course of trying to overcome difficulties. Since we feel real to the extent that a significant other confirms or ratifies our self-image, and since this ratification will serve its purpose only when it is spontaneous, only an ideal case of human relatedness could be free from paradox. The element of collusion is usually present to a greater or lesser degree, and takes the form of a bargain: You be this to me and I'll be that to you. Unless this "something for something" deal, the *quid pro quo* of a relationship (51), is accepted as part of the game of life, it is bound to lead into problems. In *The Balcony*, above all in the first act, Genet has masterfully sketched such a collusive microcosm: Madame Irma's superbrothel, in which the clients are provided with their necessary complements to change their petty existences into half-real dreams of greatness—only half-real, of course, because there is a fee for this service and also because annoying and disenchanting little slips continue to occur, for instance when the complements do not quite remember their lines. The futility of attempting change in this way and the interpersonal problems created by collusion have been dealt with in detail by Laing (64).

In general, the problems encountered in marriage therapy more often than not have to do with the almost insurmountable difficulty of changing the *quid pro quo* on which the relationship was originally based. Of course, this *quid pro quo* is never the outcome of overt negotiation, but is rather in the nature of a tacit contract whose conditions the partners may be quite unable to verbalize, even though they are extremely sensitive to any violations of these unwritten clauses. If conflict arises, the partners typically attempt to solve it within the framework of the contract, and they thus get caught in a nine-dot problem of their own making. For whatever they do within the frame is being done on the basis of group property *a*, and therefore leaves their overall pattern of relationship (the group of their relationship behaviors) unchanged. Tacit interpersonal contracts of the kind we are examining here are bound to become obsolete, if only as the result of the passage of time, and the necessary change then has to be a change of the contract *itself* (i.e., a second-order change) and not merely a first-order change within the bounds of the contract.

But, as we have already mentioned repeatedly, this step from "within" into the outside is extremely difficult. The techniques of effecting second-order change are the subject of Part III of this book.

PART THREE

Problem Resolution

7
SECOND-ORDER CHANGE

The way out is through the door. Why is it that no one will use this exit?

—CONFUCIUS

What is your aim in philosophy?—to show the fly the way out of the fly-bottle.

—WITTGENSTEIN

MYTHOLOGIES die hard, and the mythologies of change are no exception. With change such a pervasive element of existence, one might expect that the nature of change and of the ways of effecting it should be clearly understood. But the most immediately given is often the most difficult to grasp, and this difficulty is known to promote the formation of mythologies. Of course, our theory of change is yet another mythology; but it seems to us that, to paraphrase Orwell, some mythologies are less mythological than others. That is, they work better than others in their specific life contexts.

In the course of our work with human problems, as we became increasingly dissatisfied with the established mythologies and more interested in examining change for ourselves, we soon discovered what we should have expected from the outset: if anybody had bothered to look at the most obvious source for the understanding of change, he did not leave a written record. This source is spontaneous change, by which we mean the kind of problem resolution that occurs in the ordinary business of living without the help of expert knowledge, sophisticated theories, or concentrated effort. In more than one way, this absurd situation reminded us of a famous piece of scholastic enquiry into the nature of things: at some time during the thirteenth century the University of Paris attempted to answer the question of whether oil left outside in a cold winter night would congeal by searching the works of Aristotle, rather than by looking at what real oil would really do under these circumstances.

When all this began to dawn on our Aristotelean minds, we started to spend considerable time talking to people who seemed most likely to have some practical knowledge in one or more of the three following areas: 1) the phenomena of spontaneous change; 2) the methods of effecting change employed by people less encumbered by mythologies or other professional "expertise" than we ourselves; and 3) the kinds of changes, brought about by professionals, which are unaccounted for and unexplainable by their professional theories. Our contacts thus included barmen, store detectives, spontaneously recovered neurotics, sales personnel, credit counselors, teachers, airline pilots, policemen with a knack for defusing potentially explosive situations, a few rather likable crooks, unsuccessful suicides, therapists like ourselves— and even some parents. The idea seemed good, but the results were meager. We found what in retrospect seems fairly obvious, namely that a talent for unorthodox problem resolution seems to go hand in hand with an inability to clarify in one's own mind, let alone to others, the nature of the thinking and acting that go into successful interventions. Our next discovery was that we had ourselves been using similar techniques of change, which suggested to us that there had to be some body of implicit assumptions that we were operating on. It was common for us to observe the initial session of a case and, without discussion, arrive independently at the same strategy for treatment—a strategy greatly puzzling to the frequent visitors to our Center. In trying to make ourselves clear to them, we found that we, too, were strangely unable to state the theoretical basis of our choices and actions.[1]

But even though our informants did not contribute directly to a theory of change, their examples were frequently quite useful in confirming our suspicion that spontaneous change is often a far cry from what it is supposed to be according to existing theory. For example:

On her first day of kindergarten a four-year-old girl became so upset as her mother prepared to leave that the mother was forced to stay with her until the end of the school day. The same thing happened every day thereafter. The situation soon grew into a considerable stress for all concerned, but all attempts at solving the problem failed. One morning the mother was unable to drive the child to school, and the father dropped her off on his way to work. The child cried a little, but soon calmed down. When the mother again took her to school on the following morning, there was no relapse; the child remained calm and the problem never recurred.[2]

---

[1]Eventually we realized that this state of affairs was directly linked to the hierarchical structure of all language, communication, learning, etc. As we pointed out in Chapter 1, to express or explain something requires a shift to one logical level above what is to be expressed or explained. No explaining can be accomplished on the same level; a metalanguage has to be used, but this metalanguage is not necessarily available. To effect change is one thing; to communicate *about* this change is something else: above all, a problem of correct logical typing and of creating an adequate metalanguage. In psychotherapeutic research, it is very common to find that particularly gifted and intuitive therapists think they know why they are doing what they are doing, but their explanations simply do not hold water. Conversely, many gifted writers are astounded and even annoyed at the deeper meanings that others read into their works. Thus, while the former believe they know, but apparently do not, the latter seem to know more than they are willing to acknowledge—which brings us back to Laing: "If I don't know I don't know, I think I know; if I don't know I know, I think I don't know."

[2]The obvious question arises: What would have happened if the school psychologist had had a chance to start working on this problem? In all likelihood the case would have been diagnosed a school phobia, and, depending on the psychologist's professional mythology, the dependency needs of the child, the overprotectiveness of the mother, the symbiotic aspects of their relationship, a marital conflict between the parents causing the child's behavior problem could conceivably have become the object of therapy. If at age twenty-one the daughter had run into emotional difficulties of some kind or another, she would already have had a psychiatric record reaching all the way back into childhood, and this in turn would define her prognosis as worse than otherwise. Of course, all kinds of objections can be raised about this example. The most predictable is the circular argument that the ease with which the change occurred proves that no "real" phobia was involved here. The reader who is interested in this argument is referred to Salzman (82).

The next example is that of a married couple whose love-making had become less and less frequent until they had had no sexual intercourse at all for several months preceding the following incident: They were on vacation and spent the night in the home of a friend. In the friend's guest room the double bed was pushed into a corner and could thus be approached only from one side and from the foot end, while in their own bedroom the bed touched the wall only with its headboard, and they could therefore get in from their respective sides. Some time during the night the husband, who was lying next to the wall, had to get up; he bumped against the wall on his side, then realized where he was and started to climb over his wife. As he did so, he—in his own words—"realized that there was something of value there," and they had intercourse. This somehow broke the ice, and their sex relations returned to an adequate frequency. Let us not get embroiled here in the *why* of this change, but for the purpose of our exemplification merely appreciate the fact that the change occurred as a result of a very fortuitous and apparently minor event —certainly one that would hardly have been part and parcel of a professional attempt at solving the problem.

The third example is that of a middle-aged, unmarried man leading a rather isolated life compounded by an agoraphobia; his anxiety-free territory was progressively diminishing. Eventually this not only prevented him from going to work, but threatened to cut him off even from visiting the neighborhood stores upon which he depended for his purchases of food and other basic necessities. In his desperation he decided to commit suicide. He planned to get into his car and drive in the direction of a mountaintop about fifty miles from his home, convinced that after driving a few city blocks his anxiety or a heart attack would put him out of his misery. The reader can guess the rest of the story: he not only arrived safely at his destination, but for the first time in many years he found himself free from anxiety. He was so intrigued by his experience that he wanted it to be known as a possible solution for others who suffered from the same problem, and he eventually found a psychiatrist who was interested in spontaneous remission and therefore took him seriously (3). The psychiatrist has maintained contact with him for over five years and thus has been able to ascertain that this man has not only not fallen back into his phobia, but has helped a number of other phobics with their problems.

A last example, on a different scale: During one of the many nineteenth-century riots in Paris the commander of an army detachment received orders to clear a city square by firing at the *canaille* (rabble). He commanded his soldiers to take up firing positions, their rifles levelled at the crowd, and as a ghastly silence descended he drew his sword and shouted at the top of his lungs: "Mesdames, m'sieurs, I have orders to fire at the *canaille*. But as I see a great number of honest, respectable citizens before me, I request that they leave so that I can safely shoot the *canaille.*" The square was empty in a few minutes.

Is there a common denominator to these examples? On superficial examination there is not. In the first two examples the agent of change seems to be a minor, fortuitous event; in the third example an act of desperation; and in the fourth a clever piece of mass psychology. But if we apply the concept of second-order change, these seemingly disparate incidents reveal their affinity. In each case the decisive action is applied (wittingly or unwittingly) to the attempted *solution*—specifically to that which is being done to deal with the difficulty—and not to the difficulty *itself*:

1. The mother stays on, day after day, as the only "solution" open to her to avoid the child's tantrum. Relatively successful as this is, it is a typical first-order change and leaves the overall problem unchanged and unchangeable. In the process the child's difficulty in adapting to kindergarten is compounded into a "problem"; the mother's absence on that one morning also produces an absence of the avoidance behavior, and the system reorganizes itself along a new premise.

2. The couple presumably began to encounter difficulties be-

cause of the routine nature of their sex life. Their frequency of intercourse decreased; they increasingly avoided each other; the lesser and lesser frequency worried them and led them to engage in more of the same (i.e., more avoidance). The situation arising in the friend's guest room produced a second-order change by interfering with their "solution," that is, their pattern of mutual avoidance, but this change had no bearing whatsoever on what would traditionally be considered their "real" problem.

3. In the case of the agoraphobic it becomes particularly evident that his "solution" *is* the problem. When, contrary to common sense, he stops trying to solve his problem by staying within his anxiety-free space, this termination of his problem solving solves his problem.

4. The officer is faced with a threatening crowd. In typical first-order change fashion he has instructions to oppose hostility with counter-hostility, with more of the same. Since his men are armed and the crowd is not, there is little doubt that "more of the same" will succeed. But in the wider context this change would not only be no change, it would further inflame the existing turmoil. Through his intervention the officer effects a second-order change—he takes the situation outside the frame that up to that moment contained both him and the crowd; he *reframes* it in a way acceptable to everyone involved, and with this reframing both the original threat and its threatened "solution" can safely be abandoned.

Let us recapitulate what we have so far discovered about second-order change:

a. Second-order change is applied to what in the first-order change perspective appears to be a solution, because in the second-order change perspective this "solution" reveals itself as the keystone of the problem whose solution is attempted.

b. While first-order change always appears to be based on common sense (for instance, the "more of the same" recipe), second-order change usually appears weird, unexpected, and un-commonsensical; there is a puzzling, paradoxical element in the process of change.

c. Applying second-order change techniques to the "solution" means that the situation is dealt with in the here and now. These techniques deal with effects and not with their presumed causes; the crucial question is *what?* and not *why?*.

d. The use of second-order change techniques lifts the situation out of the paradox-engendering trap created by the self-reflexiveness of the attempted solution and places it in a different frame (as is literally done in the solution of the nine-dot problem).

As far as these four principles go, enough has been said about the first; Part II of this book is devoted to it in its entirety. The second principle, the uncommonsensical nature of second-order change, has been dealt with in Chapter 2. The third principle is the one that, at least in our experience, is most strongly rejected by those professionally engaged in effecting change; it must now be dealt with in some detail.

The question *why?* has always played a central, virtually dogmatic role in the history of science. After all, science is supposed to be concerned with explanation. Now, consider the sentence: "We are not competent to explain *why* scientific thinking conceives of explanation as the precondition for change, but there can be little doubt *that* this is the case." This statement is both about the principle under examination and at the same time an example of it. The awareness of the *fact* that the question *why?* is being asked and that it determines scientific procedures and their results is not predicated on a valid explanation of *why* it is being asked. That is, we can take the situation as it exists here and now, without ever understanding why it got to be that way, and in spite of our ignorance of its origin and evolution we can do something with (or about) it. In doing this we are asking *what?*

i.e., what is the situation, what is going on here and now?[3] However, the myth that in order to solve a problem one first has to understand its *why* is so deeply embedded in scientific thinking that any attempt to deal with the problem only in terms of its present structure and consequences is considered the height of superficiality. Yet in asserting this principle within our theory of change we find ourselves in good company. It certainly is not our discovery; all we can claim is that we stumbled over it in the course of our work. Only gradually did we realize that it had been enunciated before, albeit in different contexts.

One source is Wittgenstein, whose work we have already mentioned. In his *Philosophical Investigations* he takes a very strong stand against explanations and their limits. "Explanations come to an end somewhere. But what is the meaning of the word 'five'? Meaning does not enter here at all, only how the word 'five is used" (106), he states initially, and later in the same work he returns to this theme in a formulation which goes far beyond the abstractions of the philosophy of language into territory that appears very familiar: "It often happens that we only become aware of the important *facts*, if we suppress the question 'why?'; and then in the course of our investigations these facts lead us to an answer" (109). For the later Wittgenstein, what becomes questionable is the question itself; this is an idea that has great affinity with our investigations into change, and one that he had touched upon in his most important early work, the *Tractatus Logico-Philosophicus:* "We feel that even if *all possible* scientific questions be answered, the problems of life have still not been touched at all. Of course, there is then no question left, and just this is the answer. The solution of the problem of life is seen in the vanishing of this problem" (103).

[3]It is amazing how rarely the question *what?* is seriously asked. Instead, either the nature of the situation is taken to be quite evident, or it is described and explained mainly in terms of *why?* by reference to origins, reasons, motives, etc., rather than to events observable here and now.

We need mention mathematics only very briefly. It, too, does not ask *why?* and yet is the royal road to penetrating analyses and imaginative solutions. Mathematical statements are best understood as interrelated elements within a system. An understanding of their origin or causes is not required to grasp their significance and may even be misleading.

Another area in which causal explanations or questions of meaning play a very subordinate role is cybernetics. To quote Ashby once again on the general subject of change and the concept of transformations in particular: "Notice that the transformation is defined, not by any reference to what it "really" is, nor by reference to any physical cause of the change, but by the giving of a set of operands and a statement of what each is changed to. The transformation is concerned with *what* happens, not *why* it happens" (12).

And finally, proceeding from the most abstract to the more concrete, we find support for the *what?* instead of *why?* basis of observation, analysis, and action in what may loosely be termed the Black Box approach in electronics. The term, which originated in World War II, was applied to the procedure followed when examining captured enemy electronic equipment that could not be opened because of the possibility of destruction charges inside. In these cases the investigators simply applied various forms of input into the "box" and measured its output. They were thus able to find out *what* this piece of equipment was doing without necessarily also finding out *why*. Nowadays the concept is more generally applied to the study of electronic circuitry whose structure is so complex (though still much less so than the brain) that it is more expedient to study merely its input-output relations than the "real" nature of the device.

As mentioned already, resistance to a devaluation of the *why* in favor of the *what* seems greatest in the study of human behavior. What, it is usually asked, about the undeniable fact that a person's present behavior is the result of his experiences in the past? How can an intervention that leaves past causes untouched have any lasting effect in the present? But it is these very assumptions that are most clearly contradicted by the study of actual—particularly spontaneous—changes. Everyday, not just clinical, experience shows not only that there can be change without insight, but that very few behavioral or social changes are accompanied, let alone preceded, by insight into the vicissitudes of their genesis. It may, for instance, be that the insomniac's difficulty has its roots in the past: his tired, nervous mother may habitually have yelled at him to sleep and to stop bothering her. But while this kind of discovery may provide a plausible and at times even very sophisticated *explanation* of a problem, it usually contributes nothing towards its *solution.*[4]

We find that in deliberate intervention into human problems the most pragmatic approach is not the question *why?* but *what?;* that is, what is being done here and now that serves to perpetuate the problem, and what can be done here and now to effect a change? In this perspective, the most significant distinction between adequate functioning and dysfunction is the degree to which a system (an individual, family, society, etc.) is either able to generate change by itself or else is caught in a Game Without End. We have already seen that in this latter case the attempted solution is the problem. We can now also appreciate that the

---

[4]Such empirical findings are not out of line with general considerations, if these are thought through to their logical conclusions. There are two possibilities: 1) The causal significance of the past is only a fascinating but inaccurate myth. In this case, the only question is the pragmatic one: How can desirable change of present behavior be most efficiently produced? 2) There *is* a causal relationship between the past and present behavior. But since past events are obviously unchangeable, either we are forced to abandon all hope that change is possible, or we must assume that—at least in some significant respects—the past has influence over the present only by way of a person's *present* interpretation of *past* experience. If so, then the significance of the past becomes a matter not of "truth" and "reality," but of looking at it here and now in one way rather than another. Consequently, there is no compelling reason to assign to the past primacy or causality in relation to the present, and this means that the re-interpretation of the past is simply one of many ways of possibly influencing present behavior. In this case, then, we are back at the only meaningful question, i.e., the pragmatic one: How can desirable change of present behavior be produced most efficiently?

search for the causes in the past is just one such self-defeating "solution." In psychotherapy it is the myth of knowing this *why* as a precondition for change which defeats its own purpose. The search for causes—by therapist, patient, or both—can lead only to more of the same searching if the insight gained thereby is not yet "deep" enough to bring about change through insight. But neither the little girl going to kindergarten nor her parents acquired or even needed any understanding of the problem which they had for a while. Similarly, the spontaneous remission of the agoraphobia occurred without any insight into the origin and meaning of the symptom either before, during, or after the change; nor, apparently, did this man ever arrive at a deeper understanding of the theoretical nature of the help he was then able to extend to his fellow sufferers.

We can now formulate some first practical instances of second-order change. To return once more to the example of the insomniac: We have already mentioned how he became a patient by mishandling an everyday difficulty and how this mishandling placed him into a self-imposed "Be spontaneous!" paradox. Many of these sufferers can be helped quite rapidly by some seemingly absurd, paradoxical injunction, such as to lie in bed and not to close their eyes until they are fast asleep. Obviously, such an intervention does not get at the original sleeplessness, but effects a change at the *meta*level where the insomniac's counterproductive attempts at solving the problem have created his "Be spontaneous!" paradox (and where it is perpetuated additionally by medication and all sorts of "common-sense" measures). Unless the insomniac is proficient in self-hypnosis (in which case he probably would not be an insomniac), he cannot *not* wish to fall asleep, just as it is impossible *not* to think of a given thing deliberately, and this mental activity then paradoxically prevents sleep. The goal of the second-order change intervention, therefore, is to prevent him from willing himself to fall asleep, and not, as common sense would suggest, to make him fall asleep.

Or let us consider the example of a phobic who cannot enter

a crowded, brightly lit department store for fear of fainting or suffocating. Originally he may have experienced nothing worse than a temporary indisposition, a fortuitous hypoglycemia, or a vertigo as he went into the store. But when, a few days later, he was about to enter the store again, the memory of this incident may still have been fresh, and he probably "pulled himself to-gether" to brace himself against a possible recurrence of the original panic; as a result, the panic promptly struck again. Under-standably, such a person experiences himself as being at the mercy of internal forces of such overwhelming spontaneity that his only defense seems complete avoidance of the situation, probably ac-companied by the regular use of tranquilizers. But not only is avoidance no solution, not only does it merely perpetuate the conditions against which it is used, it *is* the problem, and he is caught in a paradox. He can be helped by the imposition of a counter-paradox, for instance by telling him to walk into the store and to faint on purpose, regardless of whether his anxiety is at that moment actually overwhelming him or not. Since he would have to be somewhat of a yogi to accomplish this, he can next be instructed to walk as far into the store as he wants, but to make sure to stop one yard short of the point where his anxiety would overwhelm him.[5] In either case the intervention is directed at the attempted solution, and change can then take place.[6] Similarly— although nobody can as yet present any evidence for this—it is a fair guess that the legalization of marijuana (whose ill effects are not certain, but probably not worse than those of many other widely used drugs) might not only decrease its use, but would

[5] We wish to mention only in passing that patients not only accept such absurd and often outlandish behavior prescriptions, but often do so with a big smile, as if somehow they had caught on to the essentially humorous—yet, of course, deeply serious—nature of paradox.

[6] It may seem a somewhat far-fetched comparison, but the avoidance behavior of the phobic is essentially analogous to the prohibition of pornography: both make a "problem" out of a difficulty, and in both cases the "problem" disappears together with the "solu-tion."

eliminate almost overnight the complex and counterproductive consequences of its legal suppression, which many experts feel has turned into a cure that is worse than the disease.

The elusive interpersonal phenomenon of trust provides another example of the technique by which second-order change can be applied. For example, the ideal relationship of a probationer to his probation officer should be one of complete trust since, again ideally, the probation officer is supposed to be his helper, and to fulfill his function he needs to know exactly what sort of life his client is leading. But they both know only too well that the probation officer also represents the authority of the State and thus has no choice but to report the probationer in case the latter violates any of the conditions of his probation. This being so, it would create little credence if he told his client, "You should trust me." Obviously trust is something spontaneous that one can neither obtain nor produce on demand. In training probation officers in the use of paradoxical techniques for problem resolution we have found it very useful to have the probation officer tell his probationer: "You should never fully trust me or tell me everything." The reader will readily see the similarity between his injunction and Epimenides' statement, or the claim by the sophist that he entered the kingdom to be hanged, except that in this case the outcome is not an infinite regress of assertion and denial, but the pragmatic resolution of an otherwise hopelessly paradoxical state of affairs. The probation officer's statement makes him trustworthy to the extent that he has declared himself untrustworthy, and the basis for a workable relationship is laid.

Another variation of the theme of trust and of the problem caused by the wrong handling of a difficulty can be found in Khrushchev's (perhaps apocryphal) memoirs, where he describes the defection of Stalin's daughter. After complaining how wrong it had been for her to run away to the West, he points to the other side of the story:

She did something stupid, but Svetlanka was dealt with stupidly, too—stupidly and rudely. Apparently, after her husband's funeral she went to our embassy in New Delhi. Benediktov was our ambassador there. I knew him. He's a very straightlaced person. Svetlanka said she wanted to stay in India for a few months, but Benediktov advised her to return immediately to the Soviet Union. This was stupid on his part. When a Soviet ambassador recommends that a citizen of the Soviet Union return home immediately, it makes the person suspicious. Svetlanka was particularly familiar with our habits in this regard. She knew it meant she wasn't trusted.

And Khrushchev then shows that he knows a good deal about how to handle such problems of trust in a paradoxical way:

What do I think should have been done? I'm convinced that if she had been treated differently, the regrettable episode would never have happened: When Svetlanka came to the embassy and said that she had to stay in India for two or three months, they should have told her, "Svetlana Iosifovna, why only three months? Get a visa for a year or two or even three years. You can get a visa and live here. Then, whenever you are ready, you can go back to the Soviet Union." If she had been given freedom of choice, her morale would have been boosted. They should have shown her that she was trusted. . . . And what if we had acted the way I think we should have and Svetlanka still hadn't returned home from India? Well, that would have been too bad but no worse than what happened (56).

All these examples have an identical structure: an event *(a)* is about to take place, but *a* is undesirable. Common sense suggests its prevention or avoidance by means of the reciprocal or opposite, i.e., not-*a* (in accordance with group property *d*), but this would merely result in a first-order change "solution." As long as the solution is sought within this dichotomy of *a* and not-*a*, the seeker is caught in an *illusion of alternatives* (99), and he remains caught whether he chooses the one or the other alternative. It is precisely this unquestioned illusion that one *has* to make a choice between *a* and not-*a*, that there is no other way out of the dilemma, which perpetuates the dilemma and blinds us to the solution which is available at all times, but which contradicts common sense. The formula of second-order change, on the other hand, is "not *a* but also *not* not-*a*." This is an age-old principle that was, for instance, demonstrated by the Zen master Tai-Hui when he showed his monks a stick and said: "If you call this a stick, you affirm; if you call it not a stick, you negate. Beyond affirmation and negation, what would you call it?" This is a typical Zen *koan*, designed to force the mind out of the trap of assertion and denial and into that quantum jump to the next higher logical level called *sátori*. This is, presumably, also what St. Luke meant when he wrote: "Whosoever shall seek to save his life, shall lose it; and whosoever shall lose his life shall preserve it." Philosophically the same principle is the basis of Hegelian dialectics, with its emphasis on the process that moves from an oscillation between thesis and antithesis to the synthesis transcending this dichotomy. The way out of the fly bottle, to return to Wittgenstein's aphorism (108), is through the least obvious opening. On the poetic level we find a particularly clear example of this principle in Chaucer's tale of the wife of Bath: a young knight finds himself in worse and worse predicaments as the result of having to choose again and again between two unacceptable alternatives, until he finally chooses not to choose, that is, to reject *choice itself*. The knight therefore finds the way out of the fly bottle and achieves a second-order change by switching to the next-higher logical level; instead of continuing to choose one alternative (i.e., one member of the class of alternatives) as the lesser evil, he eventually questions and rejects the whole idea that he *has* to choose and thereby deals with the class (*all* alternatives) and not just one member (95).

This is the essence of second-order change.

The most amazing thing about this kind of problem resolution is that it is possible even—or especially—where the concrete facts of the situation are immutable. To illustrate this, we must now turn to the fourth principle of second-order change mentioned earlier, namely the technique of *reframing*.

8
THE GENTLE ART OF REFRAMING

QUESTION: *What is the difference between an optimist and a pessimist?*
ANSWER: *The optimist says of a glass that it is half full; the pessimist says of the same glass that it is half empty.*

—ANONYMOUS

Life makes sense
and who could doubt it,
if we have
no doubt about it.

—PIET HEIN, *Grooks*

IT is Saturday afternoon, holiday time for all boys, except Tom Sawyer, who has been sentenced to whitewash thirty yards of board fence nine feet high. Life to him seems hollow, and existence but a burden. It is not only the work that he finds intolerable, but especially the thought of all the boys who will be coming along and making fun of him for having to work. At this dark and hopeless moment, writes Mark Twain, an inspiration bursts upon him! Nothing less than a great, magnificent inspiration. Soon enough a boy comes in sight, the very boy, of all boys, whose ridicule he had been dreading most:

"Hello, old chap, you got to work, hey?"
"Why, it's you, Ben! I warn't noticing."
"Say—I'm going a-swimming, *I* am. Don't you wish you could? But of course you'd druther *work*—wouldn't you? Course you would!"
Tom contemplated the boy a bit, and said:

"What do you call work?"

"Why, ain't *that* work?"

Tom resumed his whitewashing, and answered carelessly:

"Well, maybe it is, and maybe it ain't. All I know, is, it suits Tom Sawyer."

"Oh come, now, you don't mean to let on that you *like* it?"

The brush continued to move.

"Like it? Well, I don't see why I oughtn't to like it. Does a boy get a chance to whitewash a fence every day?"

That put the thing in a new light. Ben stopped nibbling his apple. Tom swept his brush daintily back and forth—stepped back to note the effect—added a touch here and there—criticized the effect again—Ben watching every move and getting more and more interested, more and more absorbed.

Presently he said:

"Say, Tom, let *me* whitewash a little."

By the middle of the afternoon, the fence has three coats of whitewash and Tom is literally rolling in wealth: one boy after another has parted with his riches for the privilege of painting a part of the fence. Tom has succeeded in *reframing* drudgery as a pleasure for which one has to pay, and his friends, to a man, have followed this change of his definition of reality.

In the French film *Carnival in Flanders*, the invincible Spanish forces are advancing on a small but prosperous Flemish village. A Spanish emissary rides in and conveys to the assembled burghers an order to surrender the village or have it pillaged and destroyed. He then leaves without waiting for their reply. The burghers are terrified, realizing that neither they nor their defenses are a match for the invading army. And yet, there is only one reasonable recourse—to defend their village as best they can rather than surrender it to the notorious Spanish forces and watch helplessly as their women are raped and their wealth looted. They are thus caught in a typical illusion of alternatives and can see no less disastrous solution.

But the women come up with an altogether different, rather

"insane" plan that completely reframes the situation: the men will "flee" the village, "abandoning" the women to their fate; there will be neither fight nor surrender, since there will be no men to do either. There will only be a village of helpless women in need of protection by brave soldiers—a situation that could hardly appeal more to the proverbial gallantry of the Spaniards.

Indeed, on finding themselves warmly welcomed by the women, the conduct of the "conquering forces" far exceeds the modest hopes of the villagers; they show the women valorous protection and respect, although combined with many gallant amorous adventures (which are not at all to the displeasure of the ladies). As they have to continue on their northward advance, the Spanish are sentimentally reluctant to leave their charming hostesses, and they bestow enormous gifts on the village in gratitude for such delightful and civilized hospitality.

And now for an example from our work: For reasons irrelevant to our presentation, a man with a very bad stammer had no alternative but to try his luck as a salesman. Quite understandably this deepened his life-long concern over his speech defect. The situation was reframed for him as follows: Salesmen are generally disliked for their slick, clever ways of trying to talk people into buying something they do not want. Surely, he knew that salesmen are trained to deliver an almost uninterrupted sales talk, but had he ever really experienced how annoying it is to be exposed to that insistent, almost offensive barrage of words? On the other hand, had he ever noticed how carefully and patiently people will listen to somebody with a handicap like his? Was he able to imagine the incredible difference between the usual fast, high-pressure sales talk and the way he would of necessity communicate in that same situation? Had he ever thought what an unusual advantage his handicap could become in his new occupation? As he gradually began to see his problem in this totally new—and, at first blush, almost ludicrous—perspective, he was especially instructed to maintain a high level of stammering, even if in the course of his work, for reasons quite unknown to him, he should begin to feel a little more at ease and therefore less and less likely to stammer spontaneously.

To reframe, then, means to change the conceptual and/or emotional setting or viewpoint in relation to which a situation is experienced and to place it in another frame which fits the "facts" of the same concrete situation equally well or even better, and thereby changes its entire meaning.[1] The mechanism involved here is not immediately obvious, especially if we bear in mind that there is change while the situation itself may remain quite unchanged and, indeed, even unchangeable. What turns out to be changed as a result of reframing is the meaning attributed to the situation, and therefore its consequences, but not its concrete facts—or, as the philosopher Epictetus expressed it as early as the first century A.D., "It is not the things themselves which trouble us, but the opinions that we have about these things."[2] The word *about* in this quotation reminds us that any opinion (or view, attribution of meaning, and the like) is *meta* to the object of this opinion or view, and therefore of the next higher logical level. In terms of the Theory of Logical Types this fact seems obvious enough, but applied consistently to human behavior and human problems it opens a veritable Pandora's box concerning the glibly used and usually unquestioned concept of "reality adaptation" as a criterion of normality. Which reality is the supposedly sane person adapted to? To try to answer this question exhaustively

---

[1]Reframing plays an important role in humor, except that there the second frame, usually introduced by the punchline, is a *non sequitur* that unexpectedly gives the whole story a funny slant. (As already mentioned, Koestler (59) has written extensively on this subject.) An old joke illustrating this technique goes back to 1878, when Austro-Hungary occupied Bosnia very much against the will of the Bosnians, who soon began to show their displeasure by sniping at Austrian officials. The situation grew so bad that according to an untrue story, a Draconian law was drafted in Vienna which read: For shooting at the Minister of the Interior: two years hard labor; for shooting at the Foreign Minister: three years hard labor; for shooting at the War Minister: four years hard labor. *The Prime Minister must not be shot at all.*

[2]Or cf. Shakespeare: "There is nothing either good or bad, but thinking makes it so."

would go beyond the purpose of this book, since it would lead deeply into philosophical and linguistic problems. We shall therefore sidestep the issue and merely contend that when the concept of reality is referred to in psychiatric discourse, this is rarely the reality of a thing *per se*, i.e., its basic properties, if such do exist, or even what is simply observable, though this is the *ostensible* subject. Rather, the "reality" referred to concerns "opinions" in Epictetus' sense, or, as we would prefer to put it, the meaning[3] and value attributed to the phenomenon in question. This is a far cry from the simplistic but widespread assumption that there is an objective reality, somewhere "out there," and that sane people are more aware of it than crazy ones. On reflection it becomes obvious that anything is real only to the extent that it conforms to a *definition* of reality—and those definitions are legion.[4] To employ a useful oversimplification: real *is* what a sufficiently large number of people have agreed to *call* real[5]—except that this fact is usually forgotten; the agreed-upon definition is reified (that is, made into a "thing" in its own right) and is eventually experienced as that objective reality "out there"[6] which apparently

[3]Such "meaning" is not just a matter of intellectual, objective understanding, but of the *entire personal significance* of the situation in question.

[4]Of course, this is by no means limited to humans. "A territory, for example, cannot exist in nature," writes Ardrey; "it exists in the mind of the animal" (7).

[5]For instance, the reality of a banknote does not reside primarily in the fact that it is a rectangular piece of paper with certain markings, but rather in the interpersonal convention that it is to have a certain value. An intriguing example was reported to Bateson (21) by the inhabitants of a certain coastal area of New Guinea who use shell money for small, everyday purchases, but heavy millstone-shaped rock tokens for larger transactions. One day such a stone was being transported from one village to another across a river estuary when the boat capsized in the rough surf and the "money" disappeared forever in the deep water. Since the incident was known to everybody concerned, the stone continued to be used as legal tender in many subsequent transactions, although strictly speaking its reality now existed only in the minds of a large group of people.

[6]This process of first "creating" a reality and then "forgetting" that it is our own creation and experiencing it as totally independent from ourselves was already known to Kant and Schopenhauer. "This is the meaning of Kant's great doctrine," writes Schopenhauer in *The Will in Nature*, "that teleology [the study of evidences of design and purpose in nature] is brought into nature only by the intellect, which thus marvels at a miracle that it has created itself in the first place. It is (if I may explain so sublime a matter by

only a madman can fail to see. Admittedly, there are degrees of reification: there are many situations which most people will consider "really" dangerous and, therefore, to be avoided, but even in these extreme cases we find exceptions; after all, there are people who deliberately seek their deaths, or who *want* to be eaten by the lions, or who are confirmed masochists—and these people evidently have defined reality in very idiosyncratic ways which for them are real.

Reframing operates on the level of *meta*reality, where, as we have tried to point out, change can take place even if the objective circumstances of a situation are quite beyond human control. Again the Theory of Logical Types permits us to conceptualize this more rigorously: As we have seen, classes are exhaustive collections of entities (the members) which have specific characteristics common to all of them. But membership in a given class is very rarely exclusive. One and the same entity can usually be conceived as a member of different classes. Since classes are not themselves tangible objects, but concepts and therefore constructs of our minds, the assignment of an object to a given class is learned or is the outcome of choice, and is by no means an ultimate, immutable truth. Truth, as Saint-Exupéry remarked, is not what we discover, but what we create. A red wooden cube can be seen as a member of the class of all red objects, of the class of cubes, of the class of wooden objects, of the class of children's toys, etc.[7] Moreover, in Epictetus' sense, further class member-

a trivial simile) the same as if the intellect were astonished at finding that all multiples of nine again yield nine when their single figures are added together, or else to a number whose single figures again add up to nine; and yet it has itself prepared this miracle in the decimal system" (84).

[7]Premack and Premack have presented very interesting experimental proof for the intuitively plausible assumption that animals also order their world into members and classes, and are consequently capable of distinguishing between the two. Their chimpanzee Sarah displayed this ability to a remarkable extent: ". . . the chimpanzee has been taught to sort pictures into classes: animate and inanimate, old and young, male and female. Moreover, the animal can classify the same item in different ways depending on the alternatives offered. Watermelon is classified as fruit in one set of alternatives, as food

ships of any object are determined by the "opinions" that we have about it, i.e., the meaning and value which we have attributed to it. Which of these membership attributions is considered, overlooked, preferred, feared, etc., is very much the outcome of choice and circumstance, but once something is seen as having a particular meaning or value, it is very difficult to see that same something in terms of its membership in another, equally valid class. For instance, most people detest horsemeat, but some like it. In either case it is the same thing, horsemeat, but its meaning and value, its class membership is very different for the two types of people. Only as the result of drastically changed circumstances (war, famine, etc.) may horsemeat change its metareality and become a delicacy also for those who under normal circumstances shuddered at the thought of eating it.

The reader who has had the patience to follow us through these rather tedious considerations will by now see their relevance to reframing as a technique for achieving second-order change: In its most abstract terms, reframing means changing the emphasis from one class membership of an object[8] to another, equally valid class membership, or, especially, introducing such a new class membership into the conceptualization of all concerned. If, again, we resist the traditional temptation of asking *why* this should be so, we can then see *what* is involved in reframing:

1. Our experience of the world is based on the categorization of the objects of our perception into classes. These classes are mental constructs and therefore of a totally different order of reality than the objects themselves. Classes are formed not only on the basis of the physical properties of objects, but especially

---

in another set and as big in a third set. On the basis of these demonstrated conceptual abilities we made the assumption that the chimpanzee could be taught not only the names of specific members of a class but also the names for the classes themselves (79)." Further experiments proved the correctness of this assumption.

[8] *Object* should be taken in its most abstract connotation, as including events, situations, relationships between people and between people and objects, patterns of behavior, etc.

on the strength of their meaning and value for us.

2. Once an object is conceptualized as the member of a given class, it is extremely difficult to see it as belonging also to another class. This class membership of an object is called its "reality"; thus anybody who sees it as the member of another class must be mad or bad. Moreover, from this simplistic assumption there follows another, equally simplistic one, namely that to stick to this view of reality is not only sane, but also "honest," "authentic," and what not. "I cannot play games" is the usual retort of people who are playing the game of not playing a game, when confronted with the possibility of seeing an alternative class membership.

3. What makes reframing such an effective tool of change is that once we do perceive the alternative class membership(s) we cannot so easily go back to the trap and the anguish of a former view of "reality." Once somebody has explained to us the solution of the nine-dot problem, it is almost impossible to revert to our previous helplessness and especially our original hopelessness about the possibility of a solution.

It seems that the first to draw attention to this—albeit in the context of games and the awareness of rules—was again Wittgenstein. In his *Remarks on the Foundations of Mathematics* he writes:

Let us suppose, . . . that the game is such that whoever begins can always win by a particular simple trick. But this has not been realized; —so it is a game. Now someone draws our attention to it;—and it stops being a game.

What turn can I give this, to make it clear to myself?—For I want to say: "and it stops being a game"—not: "and we now see that it wasn't a game."

That means, . . . the other man did not *draw our attention* to anything; he taught us a different game in place of our own.—But how can the new game have made the old one obsolete?—We now see something different, and can no longer naïvely go on playing.

On the one hand the game consisted in our actions (our play) on the board; and these actions I could perform as well now as before. But on the other hand it was essential to the game that I blindly tried to win; and now I can no longer do that (104).

It is not surprising that very similar conclusions should eventually have begun to surface in the mathematical Theory of Games, since rule awareness, as we have just seen, plays a decisive role in the outcome of a game. Starting from similar premises, Howard has presented a game-theoretical model of what he calls the "existentialist axiom" (46) and has shown that, indeed, "if a person comes to 'know' a theory about his behavior, he is no longer bound by it but becomes free to disobey it" (47), and ". . . a conscious decision maker can always choose to disobey any theory predicting his behavior. We may say that he can always "transcend" such a theory. This indeed seems realistic. We suggest that among socio-economic theories, Marxian theory, for example, failed at least partly because certain ruling class members, when they became aware of the theory, saw that it was in their interest to disobey it" (48).

Ashby, referring to the same subject in his *Introduction to Cybernetics*, writes: "If the reader feels that these studies are somewhat abstract and devoid of applications, he should reflect on the fact that the theories of games and cybernetics are simply the foundations of the theory of How to get your Own Way. Few subjects can be richer in applications than that! (14).

So much for the theoretical background of reframing; now for some practical examples:

One windy day . . . a man came rushing around the corner of a building and bumped hard against me as I stood bracing myself against the wind. Before he could recover his poise to speak to me, I glanced elaborately at my watch and courteously, as if he had enquired the time of day, I stated, "It's exactly ten minutes of two," though it was actually closer to 4:00 P.M., and walked on. About half a block away, I turned and saw him still looking at me, undoubtedly still puzzled and bewildered by my remark (44).

This is how Erickson described the incident that led him to the development of an unusual method of hypnotic induction which he later called the Confusion Technique. What had taken place? The incident of bumping into each other had created a context in which the obvious conventional response would have been mutual apologies. Dr. Erickson's response suddenly and unexpectedly redefined that same context as a very different one, namely, one that would have been socially appropriate if the other man had asked him the time of day, but even that would have been bewildering because of the patent incorrectness of the information, in contrast to the courteous, solicitous manner in which it was given. The result was confusion, unalleviated by any further information that would have re-organized the pieces of the puzzle into an understandable new frame of reference. As Erickson points out, the need to get out of the confusion by finding this new frame makes the subject particularly ready and eager to hold on firmly to the next piece of concrete information that he is given. The confusion, setting the stage for reframing, thus becomes an important step in the process of effecting second-order change and of "showing the fly the way out of the fly-bottle."

In a more general sense one can say that reframing is involved in all successful trance work; in fact, the ability to reframe whatever a subject does (or does not do) as a success and as evidence that his trance is deepening is the hallmark of a good hypnotist. If, for instance, hand levitation can be induced, this is an obvious sign that the subject is entering a trance. But if the hand does not move and remains heavy, this can be framed to prove that he is already so deeply relaxed as to be ready to go to even deeper levels. If a levitated hand begins to come down again, this movement can be reframed as evidence that his relaxation is increasing and that the moment the hand again touches the arm rest of the chair he will be twice as deeply in a trance as some time before. If, for whatever reason, a subject threatens to interrupt the induction by laughing, he can be complimented for the fact that not even in a trance does he lose his sense of humor; if somebody claims that he was not in a trance, this can be reframed as the reassuring proof that in hypnosis nothing can happen against a person's will. Every single one of these many possible interventions thus stands in the service of preparing, inducing, or strengthening hypnotic relaxation.

But as shown already in the preceding pages, reframing need not have anything to do with hypnosis. Erickson (29) was once faced with one of those seemingly hopeless impasses in which each partner in a relationship demands that the other yield. In the case of this couple, the spouses invariably got into an argument when preparing to drive home after a party. Both would claim the right to drive the car, and both would justify it by alleging that the other was too drunk to drive. Neither was willing to be "defeated" by the other. Erickson suggested that one of them drive the car to within one block from their home and that the other then take over and drive the car all the way to their house. With the help of this face-saving and only seemingly childish reframing the impasse was resolved.

In Chapter 6 we mentioned frigidity and the self-defeating "Be spontaneous!" paradox usually injected into the situation by both partners. As long as the problem is seen as a physiological and/or emotional symptom, this conceptual frame itself precludes the solution. The symptom is then either something which one has no way to control, or something that one should overcome by will power, and the use of will power then leads to more of the same problem. Successful reframing must lift the problem out of the "symptom" frame and into another frame that does not carry the implication of unchangeability. Of course, not just any other frame will do, but only one that is congenial to the person's way of thinking and of categorizing reality. For instance, we doubt that any therapeutic effect can be achieved by the traditional definition of frigidity as evidence of the female's hostility toward the male. This merely reframes some sort of madness (e.g., an emotional handicap) by a form of badness (her hostility), and can serve only to produce guilt and to antagonize the partners even further. If hostility is really involved, it can be utilized by reframing the problem as one produced by her overprotecting the male: Is she perhaps afraid that he would not know how to cope with the impact of her uninhibited sexuality? How can she be certain that he would not be shocked? What if he became impotent? With all these uncertainties, is it not much kinder for her to protect his ego and let him believe that there is something the matter with her rather than with him? Since this reframing is done in the presence of both spouses, one can then turn to him and speculate that, on the other hand, he does not seem to be the kind of man who would necessarily need this protection. Since (always assuming that she does indeed feel hostile) protecting him at her expense is the last thing she would be willing to do, this reframing of her problem utilizes her hostility as an incentive to prove to her husband (and the therapist) that she has no intention of protecting him and of assuming the patient role. It also challenges his virility and is likely to make him claim that he does not need her protection and that it would be quite desirable for him if she would let go of her inhibition.

A somewhat similar form of reframing can be used with the frequent conflict generated by the nagging wife and the passive-aggressively withdrawing husband. Her behavior can be re-labeled as one which, on the one hand, is fully understandable in view of his punitive silence, but which, on the other hand, has the disadvantage of making him look very good to any outsider. This is because the outsider would naïvely compare his behavior to hers and would only see his quiet, kind endurance, his forgiveness, the fact that he seems to function so well in spite of the very trying home situation to which he has to return every evening, etc. It is the very inanity of this redefinition of her behavior which will motivate her to stop "building him up" in the eyes of others at her expense; but the moment she does less of the same, he is likely to withdraw less, and nothing ultimately convinces like success.

These examples are meant to show also that successful reframing needs to take into account the views, expectations, reasons, premises—in short, the conceptual framework—of those whose problems are to be changed. *"Take what the patient is bringing you"* is one of Erickson's most basic rules for the resolution of human problems. This rule stands in sharp contrast to the teachings of most schools of psychotherapy, which either tend to apply mechanically one and the same procedure to the most disparate patients, or find it necessary first to teach the patient a new language, to have him begin to think in terms of this new language, and then to attempt change by communicating in this language. By contrast, reframing presupposes that the therapist learn the *patient's* language, and this can be done much more quickly and economically than the other way around. In this approach it is the very resistances to change which can best be utilized to bring it about. In more than one sense this form of problem resolution is similar to the philosophy and technique of judo, where the opponent's thrust is not opposed by a counter-thrust of at least the same force, but rather accepted and amplified by yielding to and going with it. This the opponent does not expect; he is playing the game of force against force, of more of the same, and by the rules of his game he anticipates a counter-thrust and not a different game altogether. Reframing, to use Wittgenstein's language once again, does not *draw the attention* to anything—does not produce insight—but *teaches a different game*, thereby making the old one obsolete. The other "now sees something different and can no longer naïvely go on playing." For instance, the pessimist is habitually engaged in an interpersonal "game" in which he first elicits the optimistic views of others, and as soon as he has succeeded in this, he challenges their optimism by increased pessimism, whereupon they are likely to try more of the same or eventually give up—in which latter case the pessimist has "won" another round, though at a loss to himself. This pattern changes drastically the moment the other person turns more pessimistic than the pessimist himself. Their interaction, then, is no longer a case of *plus ça change plus c'est la même chose*, since the one group member (pessimism) is no longer combined with its reciprocal or opposite (optimism), thereby maintaining group invariance on the basis of group property *d*, but second-order change is produced by the introduction of a completely new "combination rule." To achieve this, the pessimist's own "language," i.e., his pessimism, is utilized.

Of course, all of this is not limited to therapy; imaginative problem solvers and skilled negotiators have always used these techniques. As early as 1597, Francis Bacon, in his essay *Of Negotiating*, wrote: "If you would work any man, you must either know his nature or fashions, and so lead him; or his ends, and so persuade him; or his weakness and disadvantages, and so awe him; or those that have interest in him, and so govern him. In dealing with cunning persons, we must ever consider their ends to interpret their speeches; and it is good to say little to them, and that which they least look for."

One of the most accomplished negotiators in modern history was undoubtedly Talleyrand. What he did in 1814–15 in Vienna to lift France out of a situation that could be compared only to that of Germany in 1918—a defeated aggressor, hated by the rest of Europe, to be punished, her territory to be reduced and heavy reparations to be demanded of her—has become legendary. Thanks to Talleyrand, France emerged as the real victor from the Congress of Vienna, her territory intact, her power and role on the Continent restored, and all this without the imposition of sanctions and reparations. From the beginning of the Congress, this had been Talleyrand's goal. He had then translated this goal into a variety of themes and used whichever was most congenial to the way of thinking and the outlooks of a given interlocutor. Needless to say, his contemporaries did, and historians still do, raise the typical question: Did he believe what he said, or was he perhaps "insincere"? We do not know—and concern with these alternatives may only be misleading—but a letter he wrote to Madame de Staël from Vienna closes with the words: "Adieu: I do not know what we shall achieve here; but I can promise you a noble language."

Rather than attempting the impossibly complex task of showing Talleyrand's unique ability to change his opponents' minds at the Congress of Vienna, Crane Brinton's description of how he applied his consummate reframing skill to save the *pont de Jéna* in Paris may serve as a typical example:

The allied armies had occupied Paris after Waterloo. The Prussian Blücher wished to blow up this bridge because it commemorated a battle which the invincible Prussians had somehow lost. Wellington, who had learned better than this on the cricket fields of Eton, was able to take the first steps to stop Blücher from blowing up the bridge. Talleyrand, who had perhaps always known better, was able to head him off completely by the simple expedient of re-naming the bridge the *pont de l'École militaire*. As he himself remarks, this was "a designation which satisfied the savage vanity of the Prussians, and which as a play of words, is perhaps even a more pointed allusion than the original name of Jena." The incident, insignificant enough, is fit to stand for a good deal more in Talleyrand's life and in a world which persists in giving the lie to those hopeful souls who think men do not really quarrel over words. . . . A profounder man than Talleyrand might have gone to Blücher and urged him to forgive his enemies, pointed out that the blowing up of the bridge would not be consonant with the Sermon on the Mount, that the existence of a *pont de Jéna* did not in the least injure Prussia, and a good deal more, supported by religion and common sense. Only, would that profounder man have been able to rebuild the bridge Blücher would certainly have blown up? (26)

More than one hundred years later, King Christian X of Denmark found himself in a similar situation, when in 1943 the Germans decided to apply the "final solution" to the Danish Jews, who until then had remained comparatively safe. In his talks with the king, the special Nazi emissary for Jewish questions wanted to know how the king intended to solve the Jewish problem in Denmark. To this the king is reported to have replied with cold candor: "We do not have a Jewish problem; *we* don't feel inferior." No doubt this is a good example of reframing—how diplomatic and therefore how successful it was is a very different question. But when some time later the Germans issued an order to the effect that all Jews had to wear the yellow Star of David armband, the king successfully reframed this by announcing that there were no differences between one Dane and another, that the German decree therefore applied to all Danes, and that he would be the first to wear the Star of David. The population overwhelmingly followed the king's example, and the Germans were forced to cancel their order.

A somewhat different form of reframing, more akin to the confusion technique, was used by President Kennedy at the height of the Cuban missile crisis. On Friday, October 26, 1962, Aleksandr Fomin, a senior member of the Soviet embassy in Washington, contacted John Scali, the ABC correspondent at the State Department, on an obviously exploratory, semi-official mission. He wanted to know with the greatest urgency whether the United States would be agreeable to a solution of the crisis on the basis of a supervised withdrawal of the offensive missiles from Cuba, a Soviet pledge not to re-introduce the missiles into the island, and a public pledge by the United States not to invade Cuba. This proposal was considered acceptable, and a few hours later during that same afternoon and through the same channel, the Soviet embassy was informed accordingly. On Saturday morning, however, official news came from Moscow clearly indicating that the Soviet government had changed its position and now demanded that the withdrawal of its missiles had to be paralleled by the dismantling of the U.S. rockets in Turkey. As Hilsman describes it in his book, *To Move a Nation,* Washington then resorted to what we would call an application of the confusion technique:

It was Robert Kennedy who conceived a brilliant diplomatic maneuver —later dubbed the "Trollope Ploy," after the recurrent scene in Anthony Trollope's novels in which the girl interprets a squeeze of her hand as a proposal of marriage. His suggestion was to deal only with Friday's package of signals—Khrushchev's cable and the approach through Scali —as if the conflicting message on Saturday, linking the missiles in Cuba with those in Turkey, simply did not exist. That message, in fact, had already been rejected in a public announcement. The thing to do now was to answer the Friday package of approaches and make the answer public—which would add a certain political pressure as well as increase the speed. (45)

And as the world knows, the Soviet government accepted this and did not even attempt to disentangle this deliberately created confusion.[9]

And finally, to jump back from international to interpersonal conflict, here is yet another example of the use of confusion in the service of reframing. A police officer with a special ability for resolving sticky situations in unusual ways, often involving a dis-

[9]Khrushchev's fairly detailed treatment in his memoirs of the Cuban situation does not mention the demand for the withdrawal of the U.S. missiles from Turkey at all. As far as the above-mentioned phase of the crisis is concerned, he says nothing about the Fomin-Scali contacts (which in view of their unofficial nature is not surprising); quotes Robert Kennedy as pleading almost in tears with Anatoly Dobrynin (the Soviet ambassador) for a quick solution, since the president was fearful of a military takeover; and concludes:

We could see that we had to reorient our position swiftly: "Comrades," I said, "we have to look for a dignified way out of this conflict. At the same time, of course, we must make sure that we do not compromise Cuba." We sent the Americans a note saying that we agreed to remove our missiles and bombers on the condition that the President give us his assurance that there would be no invasion of Cuba by the forces of the United States or anybody else. Finally Kennedy gave in and agreed to make a statement giving us such an assurance (57).

For Khrushchev to make the crisis appear to have been provoked by the Americans and resolved by his superior statesmanship is in itself a brilliant piece of reframing.

arming use of humor, was in the process of issuing a citation for a minor traffic violation when a hostile crowd began to gather around him. By the time he had given the offender his ticket, the mood of the crowd was ugly and the sergeant was not certain that he would be able to get back to the relative safety of his patrol car. It then occurred to him to announce in a loud voice: "You have just witnessed the issuance of a traffic ticket by a member of your Oakland Police Department." And while the bystanders were busy trying to fathom the deeper meaning of this all too obvious communiqué, he got into his cruiser and drove off. The reader will notice that in this case the effect of the reframing was achieved through a confusingly obvious communication which lifted the meaning of the situation back out of the hostile frame into which the crowd was placing it. This puts the example somewhere between Dr. Erickson's statement, "It's exactly ten minutes of two," and the episode of the French officer who managed to clear the city square by reframing the situation as one of polite concern. He resolved the problem without firing a shot by presenting to the crowd a *new* definition of the same circumstances and thus inducing the crowd to look at the situation in this new frame and to act accordingly.

9
THE PRACTICE
OF CHANGE

The uncreative mind can spot wrong answers, but it takes a creative mind to spot wrong questions.
—ANTONY JAY, *Management and Machiavelli*

IN the foregoing we have identified principles of problem formation and problem resolution. It now remains to be shown how these principles can best be applied in the practical management of human problems. In this chapter we will draw mostly on our work at the Brief Therapy Center, but even though this will give our material a definite slant towards psychotherapy, the reader will notice that most of it is equally applicable to non-clinical, non-therapeutic contexts; in fact, clinical work is, in our view, merely a special case of the much wider field of problem resolution.

Approaching a problem with the aforementioned principles in mind leads to formulating and applying a four-step procedure. The steps are:

1) a clear definition of the problem in concrete terms;

2) an investigation of the solutions attempted so far;

3) a clear definition of the concrete change to be achieved;

4) the formulation and implementation of a plan to produce this change.[1]

---

[1]Only long after we had systematized our approach in this way did we realize that we had, without blasphemic malice aforethought, plagiarized the four Noble Truths of Buddhism, namely: of suffering, of the origin of suffering, of the cessation of suffering, and

With reference to the *first step*, it is obvious that in order to be solved, a problem first of all has to be a problem. What we mean by this is that the translation of a vaguely stated problem into concrete terms permits the crucial separation of problems from pseudo-problems. In the case of the latter, elucidation produces not a solution, but a dissolution of the complaint. This admittedly does not exclude the possibility that one will be left with a difficulty for which there exists no known cure and which must be lived with. For instance, nobody in his right mind would try to find a solution to the death of a loved one, or to the scare produced by an earthquake—except perhaps some drug companies which in their product descriptions convey the utopian implication that *any* manifestation of emotional discomfort is pathological and can (and should) be combated by medication (71). If, on the other hand, a complaint is not based on a pseudo-problem, successful completion of the first step reveals the problem in as concrete terms as possible, and this is an obvious precondition in the search for its resolution.

Little more needs to be said about the *second step*. Throughout the preceding chapters, we have studied the ways in which problems are created and maintained by wrong attempts at solving a difficulty. A careful exploration of these attempted solutions not only shows what kind of change must *not* be attempted, but also reveals what maintains the situation that is to be changed and where, therefore, change has to be applied.

The *third step*, with its implicit demand for a concretely definable and practically reachable goal, safeguards the problem-solver himself against getting caught up in wrong solutions and compounding rather than resolving the problem. We have already seen how in the name of therapy a utopian goal can become its own pathology. The therapist who introduces, or who accepts

---

of the path leading to the cessation of suffering. On reflection this is not too surprising, since the basic teachings of Buddhism are eminently practical and existential.

from his patient, a utopian or otherwise vague goal unwittingly ends up treating a condition which he has helped to create and which is then maintained by therapy. It should hardly surprise him that under these circumstances the treatment will be long and difficult. If the presenting complaint is typically seen as the tip of that mythical iceberg, a negative reframing is accomplished through which an existing difficulty becomes so complex and deep-seated that only complex and deep-going procedures hold any promise of producing change. The problem-solver who subscribes to the iceberg hypothesis of human (especially emotional) problems and sets his goals accordingly is likely to create a Rosenthal effect[2] as a result of which the way toward the solution will be long, tortuous, and even dangerous. By contrast, our work has taught us that the setting of concrete, reachable goals produces a positive Rosenthal effect. The need to start a treatment with a clearly defined and concrete goal is increasingly appreciated by many therapists interested in brief interventions; cf. the numerous references related to this subject in Barten (15). But limiting the complaint against vague vastness is often not easy. As has been mentioned, many people seeking help for a problem describe the desired change in seemingly meaningful but actually useless terms: they want to be happier or communicate better with their spouses, get more out of life, worry less, etc., etc. It is the very vagueness of these goals which makes their attainment impossible. If pressed for an answer as to what *specifically* would have to happen (or stop happening) so that they would then be happier, or communicate better, etc., they are very often at a loss. This bewilderment is not primarily due to the fact that they have simply not yet found an answer to their problem, but rather that they are asking the wrong question in the first place. As Wittgenstein stated it fifty years ago, "for an answer which cannot be

---

[2]Robert Rosenthal (81) has presented experimental evidence that the opinions, outlooks, expectations, and theoretical as well as practical biases of an experimenter, interviewer, or, we would add, therapist, even if never made explicit, have a definite effect on the performance of his subjects, whether they are rats or humans.

expressed the question too cannot be expressed" (102). But in addition to seeking the "right question" and thus defining the goal in concrete terms, we also attempt to set a time limit to the process of change. We fully agree with those therapists who have observed that a time-limited course of treatment increases the chances of success, while open-ended, long-term therapies usually drag on until the patient realizes that his treatment could go on forever, and drops out. We have found that to the extent that a patient can come up with or agree with a concrete goal (no matter how big and monolithic his problem may seem to him), he is also likely to agree to a time limit—in our Center usually a maximum of ten sessions.[3]

This brings us to *step four*. The first three steps are necessary preliminaries that in most cases can be accomplished rather quickly; the actual process of change takes place in the fourth. Let us first deal with some general strategies and then, in Chapter 10, list some of the specific tactics to illustrate how our theory of change can be put into practice.

We already know two of the general principles that obtain: the target of change is the attempted solution; and the tactic chosen has to be translated into the person's own "language"; that is, it must be presented to him in a form which utilizes his own way of conceptualizing "reality."

Another general principle has already become apparent in several of the examples presented so far: that *paradox* plays as impor-

[3]Of course, the question may be raised: Out of the vast number of conceivable goals, how do we decide which is the right one? But forced into this framework of "right" or "wrong," the question is itself a good example of a wrong question, and the only answer is that we do not, cannot, and need not know. The approach we are describing is precisely not a teleological one based on the belief that there is an ultimate state of normality of which therapists *qua* therapists have expert knowledge and can therefore make the ultimate decision as to what is best for their patients. Just as in our approach the symptom is not seen as the surface manifestation of a deep, underlying problem, so the goal is not planned in conformity with some essential, Platonic idea about the ultimate meaning of life. In step two we have found out what maintains the problem here and now; to break this feedback loop is then the obvious goal—not the actualization of some philosophical abstraction of man.

tant a role in problem resolution as it plays in problem formation. Since we have discussed this role in greater detail elsewhere (96), we can limit ourselves here to a brief recapitulation:

All human problems contain an element of inescapability, otherwise they would not be problems. This is especially so in the case of those problems that are usually called *symptoms*. To refer to the insomniac once more: it will be remembered that by trying to force himself to sleep, he is placing himself in a "Be spontaneous!" paradox, and we suggested that his symptom is therefore best approached in an equally paradoxical way, namely by forcing himself to stay awake. But this is merely a more complicated way of saying that we have thereby "prescribed" his symptom; that is, we have made him actively do it rather than fight it. Symptom prescription—or, in the wider, non-clinical sense, second-order change through paradox—is undoubtedly the most powerful and most elegant form of problem resolution known to us.

The practical application of these general principles has led us to the development of a variety of interventions, and the next chapter is devoted to their exemplification. Since every one of these interventions must, of course, be devised and implemented to fit a specific problem, it is obvious that we cannot give an exhaustive "catalogue" and that the examples contained in the following pages are neither the only nor necessarily the best interventions that an imaginative problem solver who has familiarized himself with the rationale underlying these solutions could come up with. In presenting them, we are fully aware that similar techniques have been described by others, notably Erickson (43) and Frankl (36). We also want to emphasize that our purpose is not to present complete case histories in the orthodox sense, let alone to describe "cures," but simply to illustrate how our theoretical principles of change are applied practically.[4]

A word also needs to be said here about our *failures*. While we

[4]None of what follows is recommended for problem solvers who are too honest to "play games," that is, who prefer to play the game of not seeing that they are playing games.

see our general principles as usefully applicable to the whole range
of problems encountered in clinical practice and many others
beyond this, we do not claim that practical application of these
principles and related interventions leads automatically and invariably to completely successful problem resolution.[5] There are
several potential slips between the cup and the lip.

One source of failure is an unrealistic or inappropriate goal. Not
infrequently we find that our original goal has to be revised as
more information becomes available or partial change occurs during treatment. A second reason for difficulty or failure is the
nature of the intervention chosen. If a patient carries out our
instructions and no positive change results, the fault obviously lies
in the instruction. Often a careful exploration of this failure will
reveal the flaws and enable us to devise an improved plan.

The most important Achilles heel of these interventions, however, is the necessity of successfully motivating somebody to carry
out our instructions. The patient who first agrees to a behavior
prescription and then comes back saying that he did not have the
time to carry it out, or forgot, or, on second thought, found it
rather silly or useless, etc., is a bad prospect for success. Thus, one
potential source of failure is inability to present the intervention
in a "language" which makes sense to our client and which therefore makes him willing to accept and carry out the instruction.
In the preceding chapter we have pointed out the importance of
reframing in this connection. In the next chapter, under the
heading "The Devil's Pact," we shall present yet another method
for dealing with this difficulty.

[5]As an illustration we may mention the first ninety-seven cases seen in the Brief Therapy
Center and followed up between three and six months later. They covered a very wide
range of psychiatric problems, and they were seen for seven hours each, on the average.
The problem involved was fully resolved in 40 percent of these cases (by which we mean
that the established goal of treatment was reached), and significantly but not completely
improved in another 33 percent, but the remaining 27 percent were failures.

10
EXEMPLIFICATIONS

Less of the same

Let us begin our exemplifications with a situation that in and by itself is perhaps not too frequent, but that has the advantage of permitting a fairly clear exposition of our four-step procedure.

1. THE PROBLEM. A young couple requests marriage therapy because the wife feels she can no longer put up with her husband's excessive dependence on and submission to his parents. (He is their only child, thirty years old, professionally successful, and, therefore, financially independent.) The husband readily agrees with this definition of the problem, but adds that he sees no way of solving it. He goes on to explain that all his life his parents have not only taken care of his every need, but have showered him with every conceivable form of additional support (money, clothes, cars, an excellent education, extensive travels, etc.). He states that he has reached the point where any additional gift from them adds to an already intolerable burden of indebtedness, but he also knows that to reject their constant, unwanted help would be the one thing that would hurt them most, since constant giving is their idea of being good parents.

The parents were not too happy with his choice of a partner, but the marriage immediately offered them additional justification for massive interventions into his life. It was they who chose the couple's home and made the down-payment, although the couple would have greatly preferred a smaller, less expensive home in a different area. The parents also made all the decisions regarding interior decorating and even the planting of shrubs and trees in the garden. Moreover, they supplied most of the very expensive furniture, leaving the young couple practically no chance to arrange their home as they would have liked. The parents, who live in a city fifteen hundred miles away, make four yearly visits of three weeks each, which the young people have come to dread. The parents completely take over the house; the young wife is banned from the kitchen, while the mother prepares all the meals and buys mountains of groceries; she starts washing everything washable in the house and re-arranges the furniture, while the father cleans and services their two cars, rakes leaves, mows the lawn, plants, prunes, and weeds. When they all go out together, the father invariably pays for any expenses.

2. THE ATTEMPTED SOLUTIONS. The young people say they are at their wit's end. They have tried very hard but unsuccessfully to establish a minimum of independence, but even the mildest attempt to protect themselves against the parents' dominance is interpreted as a sign of ingratitude which then provokes deep feelings of guilt in the husband and impotent rage in the wife. These attempts also lead to ludicrous scenes in public; e.g., when both mother and daughter-in-law implore the supermarket cashier to accept her money and not that of the other woman, or when father and son literally fight over the restaurant check as soon as the waiter brings it to the table. In order to alleviate some of their feelings of indebtedness, the young people have also tried to send their parents an expensive gift after each visit, only to receive a still more expensive one from them by return mail. Of course, they then feel obligated to display this gift prominently in their home, although they hate the sight of it. The harder they try to gain a minimum of independence, the harder the parents try to "help" them. Thus all four are caught in a typical "more of the same" impasse.

3. THE GOAL. In this case, the often difficult task of formulating a concrete goal was relatively easy. The couple wanted the husband's parents to stop treating them like children; they wanted the right to make their own decisions even during the parents' visits, to choose their own life style—and to achieve all this without having to feel guilty for hurting and alienating the old people.

However, for the purpose of devising an optimal intervention, this formulation was still too general. We therefore asked the husband what *specifically* would have to happen to give him tangible proof that he had achieved this goal. He immediately replied that this would be the case if and when his father told him of his own accord: "You are now grown up, the two of you have to take care of yourselves and must not expect that mother and I are going to pamper you indefinitely." The bringing about of this specific change in the father's attitude was accepted as the goal of treatment.

4. THE INTERVENTION. From all this information it seemed clear to us that any successful intervention had to be carried out within the only "language" the parents could understand, namely the overriding importance of being good parents. Since one of their quarterly visits was imminent, the couple were told the following: Until their last visit they had tried to do everything in their power to give the parents as little as possible to clean, correct, and improve. This time they were to stop cleaning the house several days before the visit, permit a maximum of dirty laundry to accumulate, stop washing the cars and leave their tanks almost empty, neglect the garden, and deplete the kitchen of almost all groceries and other supplies. Any defects in the house (for example, burned-out light bulbs, dripping faucets) were to be left unattended. They were not only *not* to prevent the parents from paying for the groceries, restaurant bills, theater tickets, gasoline, etc., but were to wait calmly until the parents pulled out their wallets, and were to let them pay for all these expenses. At home the wife was to let dirty dishes accumulate in the kitchen and expect the mother to wash them; the husband was to read or to watch television while his father was toiling away in the garage or in the garden. Every once in a while he was to stick his head out of the door, check his father's progress, and ask cheerfully: "Hi, Dad, how's it going?" Above all, they were prohibited from making any attempts to get the parents to acknowledge that they (the young couple) had a right to their independence. They were to accept everything the parents did for them as a matter of course and to thank them very perfunctorily.

If the two young people had not been so upset about the situation, it would probably have been impossible to "sell" them this idea, because on the surface, far from liberating them, it seemed to push them even deeper into the misery they wanted to get out of. However, they did carry out at least part of these instructions, and when they came for their next session two weeks later, they reported that the parents had cut their visit short. Before leaving, the father had taken his son aside and told him in friendly but no uncertain terms that he (the son) and his wife were much too pampered, that they had gotten much too accustomed to being waited upon and supported by the parents, and that it was now high time to behave in a more adult fashion and to become less dependent on them.

As can be seen from the above, no attempt was made to include the parents in the sessions and to bring about a mutual understanding of the problem and all its ramifications. Instead, the intervention was directed at the young couple's attempted solution and was designed in a way that allowed the parents to continue to play the role of "good" parents—a role that they would never have relinquished anyway. Instead of overindulging the young couple, they now dedicated themselves to the equally gratifying parental task of weaning them.

Making Overt the Covert

A middle-aged man and his wife had started conjoint family psychotherapy because they were going through monotonously repetitious verbal fights which left the wife very unhappy and worried about their effect on their teenage children. It soon became apparent that the escalations of the arguments involved a sort of teamwork: the husband (who admitted that he rather enjoyed arguments and would, for instance, never fail to get into one with a waitress) would use a subtle but predictably successful provocation, and the wife would then react in a way that enabled him to lose his temper and attack her. Needless to say, she considered her reaction as the only way of defending herself against his provocation and of *avoiding* a fight. In addition, both, but especially she, were quite unaware that without this specific "avoidance" reaction on her part the escalation could not take place. While we were still pondering the most appropriate intervention into this pattern, an incident supplied a good occasion for a behavior prescription. The following is a self-explanatory transcript made from a tape-recording of the family therapy session following the intervention:

THERAPIST: Did you carry out my instructions Sunday?
FATHER: Yes.
THERAPIST: OK, tell us about that.
FATHER: I could not get anybody to cooperate with me.
THERAPIST [*to children*]: Now, for the benefit of those who don't know what I am talking about: I had a telephone conversation with your parents Sunday morning and they had had a fight and I told your father to go to this convention in San Francisco and to get into an argument there with somebody—into a real argument—because your father has stated here (he doesn't quite remember it) that probably he is looking for a fight anyway, most of the time. And I felt that it might be a very good experience if he could for once do it on an experimental basis; sort

of find out how he goes about setting the conditions for an argument. [*To father*] And you say you couldn't find anybody to cooperate with you?

FATHER: No—I mean logically, and this is—this is funny. Occasionally I get into a donnybrook with somebody, but it is spontaneous. Now, this I went about—I was going to lay out for a fight with somebody. So a friend of mine and I went and had a martini. And so—I told the guy I wanted it dry and he said, "It is dry," and I said, "Then you drink it," I said, "What kind of gin are you using? You are using a sweet gin," I said, "This isn't a dry martini," I said, "Now fix me a dry martini." And—"OK, how do you want it?"—so he fixed me up a very good martini. The first one was probably good, too. You told me to pick a fight.

THERAPIST: Yes—and he let you down. . . .

FATHER: And so he let me down, he didn't argue with me and so he fixed me my martini, and he made it just according to my specifications, and I told him, "This is much better." He said, "I'll remember." All right, you can't very well get into an argument with people you are in business with, although I have on occasion had a fight with them, but when I went into all the display rooms there, everybody said they heard I had been ill. I said to one guy, "Why didn't you send me a card?' and he said, "I thought of it and as soon as I get home, I'll send you a card." So I waited then until I was ready to get my car. I looked at the ticket and I stalled for fifteen minutes—I figured, well, I'm gonna have a fight. I stalled for fifteen minutes to go down and get my car, so that the time would go five minutes past the hour. And I went down there and I said to the guy, "How much is it?" He says, "Three and a half dollars" and I say, "It's only three bucks." So he started figuring it out and of this extra hour I was paying for, it was only five minutes, but they say it's all or any portion of an hour. They charged me fifty cents and I tried to argue with him about it. He said, "I can't argue with you; people give me trouble about this all the time—I can't do anything, write to the management." I said, "But you are the management—I'll give you three bucks even and I'll pull my car outa here." He said, "You would? I'd just write down your number and turn it in to the boss and let him handle it." On the other hand, he probably handles lots of people like me who are looking for a fight. So once again, he did not cooperate, but I made the effort—on your instructions. Maybe because I was following your instructions I did not make too good an effort. But I very carefully engineered two places that if somebody would only play it back to me, we could have had a beautiful donnybrook.

THERAPIST [*eye-fix on mother*]: If somebody had only played it back to you—yes.

FATHER: I mean, if I had gotten that guy to lose his temper, I'd have him dead. The same way with the bartender.

As can be seen from the above, the intervention had two effects. It placed the husband into a "Be spontaneous!" paradox with regard to his "spontaneous" fights, and it made the wife more aware of her contribution to their problem than any insight-oriented explanation or interpretation could have done.

Or take the frequent case of a teenager's "bad" behavior that seems to fit neatly into the marital problem of the parents. For instance, a daughter may behave in a very disrespectful, aggressive way towards her mother, and the mother then reacts to it in a way that merely escalates their mutual hostility. Quite understandably, she expects the father to assert his authority and to help her in correcting the daughter's behavior, but finds to her dismay that he is much too "lenient" when she complains about the daughter. Rightly or wrongly she may then be left with the impression that father and daughter are in a covert coalition against her, that is, that the father secretly enjoys and encourages the girl's behavior —an unprovable accusation that he would be likely to reject angrily if she were to make it. In these cases we have found it very useful to tell the father (in the mother's presence) that he can re-establish peace at home fairly easily if he is willing to do something rather strange, i.e., to reach into his pocket and to give the daughter ten cents whenever she is being arrogant to her mother. He is to carry out this instruction silently and as if it were the most natural thing, and should the daughter insist on knowing what this is all about, he is to say merely, "I just feel like giving you a dime." In making this behavior prescription, the therapist avoids getting involved in the hopeless argument over whether the father "really" feels hostile towards the mother, and whether the daughter "really" acts out this hostility to the father's secret satisfaction. The vague symbolic implications of the prescription are a form of confusion technique as far as the girl is concerned and, on the other hand, give the mother the feeling that the father is at long last doing something to help her against the daughter—although its purpose remains sufficiently unclear to prevent them from utilizing it in their arguments. As in the first example, carrying out this prescription makes overt a "spontaneous" behavior that until then was covert—not through an insight in the orthodox sense of the term, but through a specific action. But once the "game" is overt, it becomes impossible (in Wittgenstein's and Howard's sense, as quoted in Chapter 8) to go on playing it blindly.

A twenty-five-year-old man who had been diagnosed as schizophrenic and had spent most of the past ten years in mental hospitals or intensive psychotherapy was brought into treatment by his mother, who thought that he was at the verge of another psychotic break. At the time he was managing to live a marginal existence in a rooming house, taking two college courses in which he was failing. He was manneristic in his behavior and often "politely" disruptive during our sessions. As far as he was concerned, the problem was a long-standing disagreement between him and his parents about his financial support. He resented their paying his rent and other bills "as if I were an infant." He wanted his parents to give him an adequate monthly allowance, out of which he would then take care of these obligations himself. His parents, on the other hand, felt that past history as well as his current demeanor indicated that he could not handle these responsibilities and would grossly mismanage the money. They, therefore, preferred to dole out the money on a week-to-week basis, with the amount apparently depending on how "good" or how "crazy" their son seemed at the time. This, however, was never clearly spelled out, just as the son never directly expressed his anger about this arrangement, but retreated into a sort of psychotic clowning around which the mother especially took as further evidence that he was incapable of managing his own affairs. It also increased her fear that yet another expensive hospitalization might soon be inevitable.

In the presence of his mother it was pointed out to the son that since he felt outnumbered by his parents, he had every right to defend himself by threatening to cause a far greater expenditure by suffering another psychotic break. The therapist then made some concrete suggestions as to how the son should behave in order to give the impression of impending doom—these suggestions being mostly reformulations of the somewhat weird behavior the son was engaging in anyway.

This intervention reframed the son's "crazy" behavior as something over which he had control and which he could, therefore, use to his advantage; but the same reframing allowed the mother to see it as just that and be less intimidated by it. One of the results was that during their next quarrel the mother simply got angry with him; told him that she was tired of having to manage his affairs, acting as his chauffeur, etc.; and established an adequate monthly allowance for him, with which he could sink or swim as far as she was concerned. In the follow-up interview, this arrangement turned out to be working well, so much so that the son had meanwhile managed to save enough of his allowance to buy a car, which made him even less dependent on his mother.

Advertising Instead of Concealing

There exist a large number of problems whose common denominator is some kind of socially inhibiting or embarrassing handicap; either something that the person concerned cannot help doing, but should not be doing, or, conversely, something he would like to do but cannot. In these cases the definition of the problem is usually easy, and the attempted solution typically involves some counterproductive assertion of will power. In contrast to the examples mentioned in the preceding section, there is nothing covert about the problem.

Fear of public speaking provides a good example. What the person fears most is that his tension will become obvious and that he will eventually be overwhelmed by it in front of the audience. His problem solving behavior is, therefore, oriented primarily towards control and concealment: he tries to "pull himself together" and to hide the shaking of his hands, to keep his voice firm, to appear relaxed, etc. The tenser he becomes, the harder he tries, and the harder he tries, the tenser he becomes. Although "it" has not yet happened, he "knows" that next time it will, and he can visualize the imminent disaster in every detail. These, then, are the ingredients of the situation: a) a "problem", the consequence of a premise which for him is more real than reality, and b) attempted solutions, i.e., problem solving behaviors of the first-order change type, which keep the problem alive and thereby vindicate the premise which led to the problem in the first place. In traditional psychotherapy, the correct approach would have to be directed at this premise, by way of bringing about insight into its nature and origin, while considering the problem (symptom) merely as the tip of the iceberg. By contrast, the brief therapy approach is directed at the "solution"; the person is instructed to preface his speech with the statement to the audience that he is extremely nervous and that his anxiety will probably overwhelm him. This behavior prescription amounts to a complete reversal of the solution attempted so far; instead of trying to conceal his symptom, he is made to *advertise* it. But since his attempted solution *is* his problem, the problem disappears as his problem solving behavior is abandoned, and with it disappears the underlying premise without the benefit of any insight whatsoever.

Of course, it is not easy to get somebody to carry out such an instruction. Offhand, he sees no conceivable reason for doing something as contrary to his way of thinking as publicly advertising what he most wants to conceal. It is at this juncture that the ability to speak the patient's "language" becomes most necessary. To the engineer or computer man we may, therefore, explain the reason for this behavior prescription in terms of a change from negative to positive feedback mechanisms. To a client associating his problem with low self-esteem, we may concede that he is evidently in need of self-punishment and that this is an excellent way of fulfilling this need. To somebody involved in Eastern thought we may recall the seeming absurdity of Zen *koans*. With the patient who comes and signals, "Here I am—now *you* take care of me," we shall probably take an authoritarian stand and give him no explanation whatsoever ("Doctor's orders!"). With somebody who seems a poor prospect for any form of cooperation, we shall have to preface the prescription itself with the remark that there exists a simple but somewhat odd way out of his problem, but that we are almost certain that he is not the kind of person who can utilize this solution. And to types like ourselves, we may even lecture in terms of Group Theory, the Theory of Logical Types, first-order change and second-order change. . . .

As we have mentioned, advertising is the technique of choice when concealment is the attempted solution. It can therefore be used with blushing, nervous tremors (as suggested by Frankl (34, 35) many years ago), the fear of appearing boring and of having nothing to say to a person of the opposite sex (where advertising this has the additional advantage of motivating the other to be particularly kind and supportive, thereby wrecking that self-fulfilling prophecy), in frigidity as well as impotence, and with a host of similar problems. The interesting thing is that even when the subject cannot bring himself to carry out this instruction, the mere fact that it is on his mind, that he now sees a potential way out of the fly-bottle, may be enough to change his behavior sufficiently to avoid another round of his old "game"[1]—and nothing convinces like success.

The Great Effects of Small Causes

Quite a few people live in constant fear of making mistakes. More often than not, the number and gravity of their mistakes are no greater than the next person's, but this quite evident fact in no way mitigates their anxiety. However, their worries may indeed make them more prone to commit slips and errors, and it is usually their attempts at somehow preventing them which set the stage for their occurrence.

The case of a dental technician offers a typical example. For all she knew her employer considered her quite competent and was very satisfied with her services. She also readily admitted that she had not yet blundered so grossly that he would have to dismiss her. But this was only a question of time, and time was definitely running out on her, since her fear of that big mistake was becoming worse and worse and made her work (which she basically liked and which she needed for her livelihood) an almost nightmarish experience.

She was at first quite horrified when we instructed her to deliberately commit one small, inexpensive, but rather stupid mistake every day. As the reader can appreciate, this behavior prescription was, of course, directed at her problem-engendering over-cautious avoidance behavior—but for her it was a most absurd idea which could not have been more contrary to what she considered the only possible solution, namely more of the same avoidance. It was necessary to explain to her in great detail the "real" reason for the instruction, an explanation which is equally useful in other, similarly structured problem situations, like cases

[1]More about this aspect of the intervention will be found in the section entitled "The Bellac Ploy."

of psychogenic pain, compulsions, tics, bed-wetting, and a host of other seemingly uncontrollable conditions. Briefly, what this explanation amounts to is a reframing, utilizing the person's understandable wish to gain control over the symptom. We explained to her that through the sheer exercise of more will power she would probably be able to prevent the worst mistakes from occurring, but she would never feel sufficiently in control to consider herself safe. It would be a constant battle. This she sadly agreed with. We then pointed out that real control over problems like hers is achieved only when the person is capable not only of avoiding but also of creating them *at will*. Hence the need for her to follow our prescription, for only in the course of committing deliberate mistakes would she learn how to gain full control over them.

She came back and reported that she felt much better, even though in a sense things were now worse: her promise to commit that one small daily mistake and the planning that went into it were so much on her mind that she did not have time to worry about that other, big mistake. Fairly soon, however, she began to find this whole exercise rather silly, and a second-order change was eventually achieved, again without any exploration of the "deeper" reasons for her symptom and without any insight on her part.

A somewhat similar problem was presented by an attractive thirty-year-old woman whose life style could have been copied straight out of Buñuel's film *Belle de Jour*, except for the fact that she was unmarried. She enjoyed her professional career and was respected by her colleagues, who would have been utterly surprised to discover that at night this very proper person led a very different life. She would go to a bar or a cheap dance hall, manage to get picked up by some unsavory character, let him accompany her back to her apartment after a good deal of drinking, and then invariably be outraged and very frightened when he expected the obvious and she expected him to leave. From her description the matter could not be taken lightly, because some of these men had assaulted her rather brutally. However, she was unaware of how she got herself into these situations, except that she felt some compulsion to expose herself to these assaults by men whom she otherwise thoroughly despised for being socially and intellectually well below her. With this sketchy description of her problem she provided the two main themes (a murky unawareness of her own motives and a toying around with degradation) around which our intervention was designed.

We explained to her that for reasons she as well as we would probably never understand, she had a need to punish herself. Since evidently her right hand did not know what her left hand was doing, it was first of all necessary for her to become aware of the mechanism involved, and this could be done only by careful and gradual experimentation. In a slow and painstaking build-up of this theme she was eventually instructed to expose herself to social stigma and degradation in a small way, whenever she felt the renewed urge to degrade herself in a big way. Specifically, she was made to promise that she would then carry out one of a variety of behavior prescriptions, like wearing two different shoes in public or an oil smear on her face, or leaving the house with some item of clothing in visible disarray (she always dressed impeccably), or deliberately stumbling and falling in a crowded shopping center, etc.

Very much as in the case of the dental technician, it was the small but deliberate nature of the required action which brought about a change in her behavior. The thought of having to expose herself voluntarily to public ridicule and disgrace was so unacceptable that it overshadowed the rest of her behavior. Again, nothing coming anywhere near to insight was brought about; her behavior changed in the sense that she became unwilling to expose herself to great humiliation after she had discovered how dreadful it was to expose herself to small embarrassment.

Another young lady, also unmarried, was leading a promiscuous

life that made her feel very cheap but at the same time was her
only alternative to the depressing idea that otherwise no man
would care for her company. To make things worse, after every
sexual encounter she felt totally dissatisfied and therefore also
worthless as a "lay." She would then typically be too ashamed to
see that man again and would start going out with another one.
What she was unable to see was that under these circumstances
her attempts at solving her problem (i.e., to start all over again
with somebody else who again was only interested in her sexually)
actually were her problem. To get her out of this vicious cycle,
and in keeping with our rule that the therapeutic intervention
must be applied to the "solution," we instructed her to tell her
next boyfriend that for reasons which she could not possibly
reveal, but which were of a highly symbolic nature, she could
make love only if he first gave her twenty-five cents—but that it
had to be an old silver quarter and not a new alloy coin. Here, too,
we offered no explanation for this prescription. She was shocked
at its implication but on the other hand sufficiently interested in
continuing therapy, and this left her with no alternative than to
stop sleeping around, thereby discovering to her surprise that men
would not simply ditch her because she refused to go to bed with
them. In this way a change was achieved even though she never
did carry out the instruction, which leads to another form of
intervention:

The "Bellac Ploy"

An experienced, intelligent executive assistant, accustomed to
make her own decisions, was having difficulties with one of her
bosses. Judging from her own description of the conflict, this man
was apparently both annoyed and made to feel insecure by her
independent and rather forceful *modus operandi,* and in turn
missed few opportunities for putting her down, especially in the
presence of third parties. She felt so offended by this that she

tended to adopt an even more distant and condescending attitude towards him, to which he then reacted with more of the same belittling which had made her angry in the first place. The situation escalated to the point where he apparently was about to recommend her transfer or dismissal, and she was considering outdoing him by handing in her resignation.

Without explaining to her the underlying reasons, we instructed her to wait for the next incident and then to utilize the first opportunity of taking her boss aside and telling him with an obvious show of embarrassment something to the effect that "I have wanted to tell you this for a long time, but I don't know how to tell you—it is a crazy thing, but when you treat me as you just did, it really turns me on; I don't know why—maybe it has something to do with my father," and then to leave the room quickly before he could say anything.

She was at first horrified, then intrigued, and finally she found the whole idea enormously funny. She said she could hardly wait to try it out, but when she came back for her next appointment, she stated that the very next morning her boss's behavior had somehow changed overnight, and that he had been polite and easy to get along with ever since.

If proof were needed for the fact that reality *is* what we have come to *call* "reality," this form of change could help to supply it. Strictly and concretely speaking, nothing had "really" changed in the sense that no explicit communication or action had taken place between these two people. But what makes this form of problem solving effective is the knowledge that one can now deal differently with a previously threatening situation. This then brings about a change in one's behavior which is transmitted through the multiple and very subtle channels of human communication and which affects the interpersonal reality in the desired form, *even if the actual behavior prescription is never resorted to.* We have already mentioned this particular effect in the section on "advertising." Thus, while in typical human conflict situations the more things change the more they remain the same, it is almost the opposite here: the more things remain the same, the more they change.

We have come to refer to this type of intervention the *Bellac ploy,* after Jean Giraudoux's play *L'Apollon de Bellac.* Agnes, a timid girl, is nervously waiting to be called into a president's office for a job interview. Also in the waiting room is a young man who, on learning about her fears, tells her that the simplest way of dealing with people is to tell them that they are handsome. Although at first she is shocked by the apparent dishonesty of his suggestion, he manages to convince her that telling somebody that he is handsome *makes* him so, and thus there is no dishonesty involved. She follows his advice and is immediately successful with the grouchy clerk, then with the haughty vice-president, and with the directors. Eventually the president comes storming out of his office:

"Miss Agnes, for fifteen years this organization has been steeped in melancholy, jealousy and suspicion. And now, suddenly this morning, everything is changed. My reception clerk, ordinarily a species of hyena —[the clerk smiles affably] has become so affable he even bows to his own shadow on the wall—[Clerk contemplates his silhouette in the sunshine with a nod of approval. It nods back.] The First Vice-President, whose reputation for stuffiness and formality has never been seriously challenged, insists on sitting at the Directors' meeting in his shirt sleeves, God knows why . . ." (39).

The president, too, becomes a changed man as soon as Agnes tells him that he is handsome. A little later, in the presence of his quarrelsome wife Thérèse, he arrives at the most significant conclusion, namely that saying to others that they are handsome makes *oneself* beautiful:

"Have you ever stopped to wonder, Thérèse, why the good Lord made women? Obviously they were not torn from our ribs in order to make life a torment for us. Women exist in order to tell men that they are handsome. *And those who say it the most are those who are most beautiful.* Agnes tells me I'm handsome. *It's because she's beautiful.* You tell me I'm ugly. Why? (40) (Italics ours.)

What Giraudoux thus sketches is the opposite of those self-perpetuating interpersonal tangles where ugliness engenders ugliness in the other and then feeds back on itself. Giraudoux also shows, albeit with the playwright's artistic license to oversimplify, that a very small initial change may be all that is needed to effect a change of the entire pattern. And what about the Apollo of Bellac, that paragon of beauty to which all the players are compared? There is no such statue, the young man confides to Agnes; he has made it up, but everybody else is willing to believe that the Apollo exists.

Utilizing Resistance

As mentioned briefly in Chapter 8, resistance to change can be turned into an important vehicle of change. This can best be accomplished by reframing the resistance as a precondition for, or even an aspect of, change. A few examples will illustrate this.

Uncommonsensical as it may seem to the layman, quite a few people seem to enter therapy not for the purpose of resolving a problem and being themselves changed in the process, but behave as if they wanted to defeat the expert and presumably "prove" thereby that the problem cannot be solved, while at the same time they clamor for immediate help. Eric Berne has called a very similar pattern the "Why don't you—yes but" game (23). Within the context of reason and common sense, this attitude establishes a typical impasse in which somebody's demand for help leads to common-sense advice from others, to which he responds with more of the same (i.e., with more reasons why this advice cannot be used, and with more demands for "better" help), to which the others react with giving him more common-sense help, and so on. In terms of the pragmatics of human communication, they respond to him predominantly on the *content* level and ignore his communications on the *relationship* level (92)—until sooner or later, usually later, the relationship becomes so painful or frustrating that one party or the other gives up in desperation or anger.

The attitude just described can be influenced rather easily, provided the problem solver himself is willing to leave the frame dictated by common sense and reason, and ask the (only apparently absurd) question: "Why should you change?" For this shift in logical typing the complainant is usually ill prepared. By the rules of *his* game it is understood and thus unquestionable that he *should* change—in fact, his entire "game" is based on this premise. "Why should you change?" is therefore no longer a move *in* his game; it establishes a new game altogether, and he can no longer go on playing the old one. For instance, if one tells a bright, thirty-year-old schizophrenic who has spent ten years of his life in various hospitals that he should change, that he should free himself from the influence of his family, get a job, start a life of his own, etc., he may agree, but then explain that his voices are confusing him and that he simply is not ready to leave the hospital. He has heard these exhortations often enough and knows how to defeat them. A very different situation arises if one takes the why-should-you-change? approach. Instead of countering nonsense with common sense (a pair of opposites which together establish persistence rather than change), the Judo technique of utilizing the other's resistance is the method of choice: "I know I should not tell you this, because what are you going to think of a doctor who says such things; but strictly between you and me I must tell you what I really think of your situation. As far as I am concerned, it is I who should have his head examined, not you. Because you have made it, you have found a way of life which most of us would dearly love to live. When I wake up in the morning, I face a day in which ninety-nine things are likely to go wrong, I face ten miserable hours of all kinds of responsibilities and problems. And you don't even have to get up if you don't want to, your day is safe and predictable, you will have three meals served to you, you will probably play golf in the afternoon and watch a movie in the evening. You know that your parents will continue to pay for your stay in this hospital, and when they eventually die you can be certain that the State will look after you. Why on earth should you exchange your style of life for some stupid rat race like mine?" If this theme is sufficiently developed and consistently maintained, the patient will soon respond to it with something like, "What are you—some kind of a nut, doctor? I should be out of this place, have a job, and lead my own life— I am fed up with being called a patient." (Again, the reader should bear in mind that the foregoing is presented not as a "cure" for "mental illness," but as an illustration of a second-order change technique.) A variant of this intervention is the question: "How could you possibly change?"

Whenever change is slow in appearing, common sense suggests that some form of encouragement and perhaps a little push are needed. Similarly, when change does occur, praise and optimism are thought to facilitate more progress. Nothing is usually further from the truth. Incipient change requires a special kind of handling, and the message "Go slow!" is the paradoxical intervention of choice. For instance, it would be patently counterproductive to commend the above-mentioned patient for his newly found willingness to get out of the hospital and to face life. Instead, all kinds of pessimistic objections and dire predictions may now be raised by the therapist, all amounting to the warning that the patient is looking at his situation with unrealistic optimism, that his sudden hurry can only lead to disappointment, that what he is saying does not sound as if it came from him, but that he has perhaps read it in some book, and that under no circumstances should he, for the time being, let his plans go beyond the thinking stage. One might suggest that in order to let things crystallize in his mind, he should not even think about them for at least a week.

The "Go slow!" intervention may be fruitfully combined with the prescription of a relapse, especially when somebody has for the first time overcome a seemingly insurmountable obstacle and is now elated over his success but fearful that it may have been just a fluke. He may then be told that there is bound to be a relapse, that this is a desirable thing, because it will permit him to understand the nature of his problem much better, and that he should therefore help to bring about such a relapse, preferably before the next session. Within the frame of this "Be spontaneous!" paradox only one of two things can happen: either he has a relapse, in which case this event is reframed as proof that he now has enough control to produce a relapse deliberately; or he does not produce one, which "proves" that he now has enough control to avoid his problem deliberately. In either case he is again told to go slow.

Other forms of paradox have equally great potential in dealing with resistance to change. We have already referred to the probation officer's statement that the probationer should never trust him fully or tell him everything. Many years ago Aichhorn (4) recommended discussing with the juvenile delinquent how he let himself get caught and not why he broke the law. Another version of this type of paradoxical intervention was used with a middle-aged man undergoing hypnotherapy for a sleeping problem reaching back many years. From all objective signs he seemed to enter a trance quite readily, but he could never be induced into the slightest motor activity (e.g., finger movements or hand levitation), and on coming out of the trance he would invariably doubt that he had achieved a hypnotic state, his reddened sclerae notwithstanding. In very much the same way he complained at session after session that his sleeping problem had not improved, although his wife let us know that he seemed to sleep quite soundly. He was eventually told that for reasons that were too technical to explain in the short time available, and with which he probably would not agree anyway, he should never, under any circumstances, inform us of any improvement in his sleeping pattern, but simply terminate therapy "as soon as possible." He was somewhat puzzled, but agreed. Two sessions later he informed us that he was now sleeping a reasonable number of hours every night without the Seconal that he had been taking for nineteen years, and that he could now carry on by himself. We criticized his breaking our agreement of *not* letting us know and expressed some guarded pessimism about the rapidity of his change. He contacted us again three months later, stating that in the meantime he had been sleeping well without medication, but that a recent difficulty at work seemed to interfere with his sleep again. He was given a reinforcement and he called back after that session, stating that he had overcome the relapse.

A teenage boy had been suspended from school after he was caught selling barbiturates on the school grounds. He was annoyed, not so much because he would be missing school, but because his "business" would be interfered with. His annoyance became intense anger when the principal told him that the suspension was "for his own good and to help him." While he was to be suspended, the principal informed him, he would be given credit for any work he did on his own at home—homework assignments, preparing for examinations, etc.—and his mother would be allowed to pick up these assignments at school and bring them home to him. Since the boy had not been much of a student to begin with, but now was furious with the principal over the suspension, he announced to his mother that he would be damned if he would do any schoolwork. It was at this point that the mother sought help.

Her hope was that the therapist could get the boy into his office and somehow make him accept the principal's ruling so that he would not remain so angry and therefore intransigent about schoolwork. Instead, the therapist, realizing that the boy's anger with the principal afforded a lever for change, instructed the mother as follows: She was to go home and simply tell the boy that she had talked over his situation with some other mothers and had come to realize something, but that she was not sure whether she should tell him what it was. After some brief hesitation she was to go ahead and come out with this troublesome "realization": that his principal was noted for stressing the importance of students attending classes, that he believed quite firmly that a student just could not keep up with his studies without faithful attendance, and that he had probably suspended him to make him fail the entire school year. She was then to point out to the boy that if during his suspension from school he should do as well or even better on his own than when he attended class, the principal would be very red-faced and embarrassed. She was to finish this narrative by suggesting that it might be for the best if he did not "do too well," and thereby save the principal's face. The mother subsequently reported to the therapist that when he heard this, her son's face lit up with a diabolical grin and revenge shone in his eyes. He had found a way to gain retribution, and it mattered little that it would require his buckling down to work. In a follow-up session the mother reported that her son had thrown himself into the schoolwork "with a vengeance" and was beginning to get better grades than ever before.

What would seem more anti-therapeutic and callous than to tell somebody who is seeking help that his situation is hopeless? And yet, as the reader is by now aware, there is a whole class of human problems in which the common-sense, "human" attitude of optimism and support has no other result than to cement the persistence of a problem. If we again avoid the time-honored exercise in futility of asking *why* some people should play the game of signaling, "Help me, but I won't let you," but accept the fact *that* there are such people, we can concentrate on *what* they are doing, how it fits into the present context, and *what* can be done about it. A typical representative of this class of help seekers is the person who comes into therapy with a problem with which he has already defeated an impressive number of experts. With these antecedents, the therapist soon realizes that his head is destined to become the next addition to the patient's trophy board, and that under these circumstances any display of professional confidence and optimism would play right into the patient's hands, regardless of his "real" or "underlying" reasons. The therapeutic stance becomes, therefore, not "How can I help you?" but "Your situation is hopeless." The therapist prepares for this intervention by first patiently inquiring into all the details of past failures—how many doctors the patient has seen, what they unsuccessfully tried to accomplish, how many and what tests were made, what kinds of medication and surgical or other procedures were employed, and so on. Once he has amassed a considerable weight of evidence for failure, he confronts his client with this evidence in as authoritarian, condescending, and pessimistic a way as possible. He finishes by telling the patient that the latter has totally unrealistic expectations about what therapy can give him, and that there is nothing that can be done about his problem, except perhaps to teach him how to live with it. In doing this, the therapist completely changes the rules of the game; *he* is now the one who claims that therapy is of no use, and he can make this claim even more impressive by staking his professional reputation on the prediction that the patient will not change. This leaves the patient with only two alternatives: either to relinquish his game altogether or to continue it—which he can do only by "defeating" the expert through "proving" that improvement *is* possible. In either case the intervention leads to a second-order change.

Essentially the same intervention can be used with the typical sullen, recalcitrant teenage delinquent. The style of the therapist's speech is similarly condescending and obnoxious, and is mostly based on the pronouncement that the client is a "born loser" and therefore doomed to "lousing things up": "From long experience with people like you I can predict, with no uncertainty, that it will not be more than three, maybe at most six months, before you again foul up and get yourself into trouble. Your parents have the ridiculously old-fashioned notion that I or perhaps someone else can help you to lead a less stupid life. I am going to call them in and tell them to save their money—I don't like to waste my time on losers." The parents are then seen alone and the best strategy for dealing with the problem is discussed with them in the "language" which they are most ready to accept. In the following sections we shall present some of these strategies.

Unchallengeable Accusations and Unprovable Denials

There exist problem situations in which one party accuses another of certain actions for which there is no direct evidence, but for which the accused party has indeed acquired a reputation in the past. This kind of problem can be seen, for instance, by therapists or juvenile probation officers working with the families of delinquent children, or in marriages where one spouse accuses the other of excessive drinking.

The pattern looks something like this: Against a background of past "badness" (which the "accused" has acknowledged), the "accuser" suspects that the accused is secretly repeating the old offense. To this suspicion the accused responds by denying the charge. The pattern escalates when the accuser then brings up "evidence"—e.g., "Your speech was slightly slurred the other night, you looked heavy-lidded, you were unsteady on your feet, etc."; or, in the case of the teenager, "You turned red when I asked you about having sexual relations with your boyfriend," or "You rushed right up to your room when you came home," or "You have been moody," etc. On being confronted with this vague "evidence" the accused becomes angry and defends himself with more vigor, thereby convincing the accuser that such loud protestations are further evidence of guilt. Things may reach a boiling point, at which the accused then may again run away from home, or take a drink, and this can then be used by the accuser as additional tangible evidence that his suspicions were justified from the very beginning. By the time such problems are brought to a therapist, the accuser is fully convinced of the "facts" and the accused is helplessly frustrated.

In our view it is of secondary importance to ascertain the "true facts." For one thing, it is nearly impossible. But more importantly, to whatever extent the accused is indeed engaged in some form of unacceptable behavior, the accuser's method of dealing with it can only perpetuate and exacerbate the problem. And even if the accused is really behaving rather well, how can he convince the accuser, who "knows" differently?

The intervention that can often swiftly interrupt this cycle of unchallengeable accusations and unprovable denials requires that both parties be present in the session. The therapist avoids getting into any discussion about the validity of the accusation or of the defense. He sidesteps this issue by stating that since he was not there he is in no position to judge the "facts." However, he remarks that since the accused has admitted the alleged behavior in the past, at the very least the accuser has a point. Having acknowledged this point, he then goes a little beyond it by suggesting that while the accuser has some evidence, he may not be observant enough to pick up more evidence and that the immediate task, therefore, is to sharpen his perceptiveness—but this will require the accused's "help." If the problem is drinking, the accused is instructed not to drink one day but to make every attempt to appear drunk, and to drink considerably on another day but to appear as sober as he possibly can. He is also advised that he may do this more than once each time and in a random fashion. The accuser can then find out how good his or her perception is by trying to make the right diagnosis. In the case of the parents accusing their teenager of secret misconduct, the latter, in the presence of his parents, is given a brief lecture on "maturing" with emphasis on the fact that one aspect of maturing is "to keep one's own counsel." In order to develop that form of maturity he is told to do one or more things during the coming week that would please his parents and make them proud, but not to tell them anything about it. The parents, in turn, are instructed to "help" their child by testing his resolve to keep these actions a secret from them, which they can best do by pressing him for some details about these actions. If the child should feel that the parents are doing too superb a job of pressuring him, he is, as a last resort, to make up a lie about having done something bad.

As the reader will appreciate, this intervention reverses the impasse the family has created through their "problem solving" behavior. They cannot now go on playing the same old game, for it is now the task of the accuser to discover where and when the accused is behaving *well*, while the accused no longer has any reason to present unprovable denials.

Benevolent Sabotage

This is an effective intervention in the management of another one of those typical, monotonous crises between parents and their rebellious teenagers (although it is also applicable to other situations where one person is busily but ineffectively struggling to exert some control over another's behavior). In most cases the problem is easy to define: the youngster does not obey, does not study or keep his room in order; he or she is rude, ungrateful, comes home late, is about to fail at school, runs around with the wrong crowd, is probably using drugs, is about to get or has already gotten into trouble with the law, etc., etc. The situation has usually developed over time in a stereotypical fashion. The transition of the teenager from a child to a young adult is one of the several periods of change in families which require corresponding changes of their interaction rules, i.e., a second-order change. To oversimplify this point: while it may be quite sufficient to tell a child of eight, "You do what I say, or else . . ." at age fourteen he may turn around and ask nastily, "Or else what?" and the parents are then left with their old repertory of sanctions which have lost their effectiveness years ago. Common sense and the more-of-the-same recipe of first-order change can now lead only to an impasse, where the more things change the more they are the same, only worse. The parents may, for instance, first try to reason with the teenager; this fails because the premises of his reasoning are different; they then impose some minor punishment; the youngster rebels successfully; they impose more sanctions which (by the rules of group property *d*) serve only to elicit more rebelliousness, until finally the police and the juvenile authorities are called in to deal with what is now clearly recalcitrant, uncontrollable behavior.[2] Quite obviously, the attempted solutions thus create and maintain the problem, but this fact remains shrouded in the interpersonal blindness which is so typical of human conflict. The parents do not dare to relax their pressure, because they "know" the behavior of their youngster would then get totally out of hand; for him, on the other hand, rebellion is the only way of ensuring psychological survival against what in his view is the threat of their constantly rising demands. The result is a typical *punctuation* problem, described briefly in Chapter 2 in connection with group property *b*. The outside observer is left with no doubt that if either party would do *less* of the same, the other party would soon follow suit.

To this end the parents are instructed to use benevolent sabotage. This consists in taking a one-down position, based on a frank admission to the youngster of their inability to control his behavior. "We want you to be home by eleven—but if you are not, there is nothing we can do" might be one of their messages. Within this new frame the adolescent quickly finds that assertion

---

[2]Anybody working with juvenile delinquents knows that the possibilities open to these authorities are as limited as the parents', and that the juvenile very quickly recognizes them as just another set of paper tigers.

and defiance suddenly do not make much sense. One cannot very well defy the weak. The parents may then be instructed to lock all doors and windows of the house at eleven and to go to bed, so that when he eventually comes home he cannot get in and must ring the bell or knock. They have to pretend that they are fast asleep and let him wait outside for a long time before unlocking the door—but not without first enquiring in a confused state of sleepiness who he is. They are then to let him in, apologize for having let him wait in the cold, and stumble back to bed without the usual interrogation as to where he has been, why he is so late, etc. On the following morning they are not to bring the subject up again unless *he* does so, in which case they are again to take an embarrassed, apologetic attitude. To every misbehavior of the youngster they are to respond as soon as practically feasible with some additional act of sabotage: if he fails to make his bed, the mother is to make it for him, but crumble several crackers and throw them between the sheets. When he complains, she is to admit apologetically that she did eat crackers while making the bed and that she is sorry about the mess. If he never picks up his clothes, the mother is to make a stupid mistake ("I don't know what's the matter with me these days—I do one dumb thing after another") and put starch into his laundry, or salt instead of sugar into his favorite custard, or accidentally spill a glass of milk over him while he is getting ready to go out on a date. At no times must the parents sound sarcastic or punitive about these acts of sabotage, but always apologetic and distraught.

The task of making this behavior prescription palatable is easiest with those parents who are helplessly enraged at the adolescent's behavior and therefore quite willing to carry out the prescription within a frame of "getting back at him." But as the reader may imagine, other parents (especially mothers) may show greatly varying degrees of reluctance to carry out or even consider the whole idea. The unwillingness to "pretend," to "play games" is the most frequent stumbling block, followed by the protestation, "I could not possibly be that mean to him."

Before even mentioning this intervention, we must thus have a clear idea in what "language" to present it. If the parents appear to subscribe to the negative utopia of seeing life as beset by problems requiring constant sacrifices by them, they can be told that the requested behavior will be a difficult sacrifice for them, but that it is their parental duty to make this sacrifice. To the more military-minded parents it may be useful to point out that the soft-hearted drill sergeant is bound to be considered a nice pal by his recruits, but that as a result of his kindheartedness they will leave basic training ill-prepared for front-line duty and will soon be decimated, while the trainees of a tough instructor will probably hate his guts, but stand an excellent chance of surviving in combat. Somewhat the same argument can be used with those conscientious parents who want to be liked and therefore dread being "mean." They can be criticized for trying to make the business of child-rearing too easy for themselves at the expense of their children. Others are most likely to accept this task if it is explained to them that one of the most important lessons an adolescent has to learn is that one hand washes the other, and that their child obviously does not realize how much he has been getting from them without giving them much, if anything, in return.

Of course, at all times great attention has to be paid to the degree to which the parents can agree on a joint course of action. If they seem rather poor prospects for cooperation, a symptom prescription within the symptom prescription may be indicated, and they can, for instance, be told that the weaker one will probably do something quite outside of his/her awareness to wreck their chances of success, but that it is impossible to tell beforehand which of the two will turn out to be the weaker one.

A great part of the effectiveness of benevolent sabotage lies in a twofold process of reframing: it makes it useless and unappealing for the adolescent to rebel, since there is not much left to rebel against, and it turns the dynamics of the family's interaction virtually upside down. In a typical family with a juvenile delinquent the parents are overtly punitive and repressive but covertly permissive and seductive. Benevolent sabotage produces a situation in which they become overtly permissive and helpless but covertly punitive in a way against which the youngster cannot very well rebel. Instead of using empty threats, "reason," and exhortations, the parents acquire a quiet but much more powerful way of handling their child. This change interdicts a useless, problem-maintaining "solution."

The Benefits of Inattention

The degree of attention that people are willing to pay to one another is an important element of the nature of their relationship and can easily become the source of problems. But attention and its absence, inattention, are yet another pair of opposites which, when pitted against each other, invariably produce the identity member and, therefore, zero second-order change. In this context, as in the analogous examples cited already, the solution requires a shift to a premise that seemingly violates all common sense. For example:

A young, eager teacher is having difficulties with a so-called problem student. While the rest of the class seems to benefit from her teaching this child (a boy of eight years of age) does not. The teacher calls in his parents for a conference and learns that they are divorced, that the mother works and has little time for him, and that at home he leads a rather lonely life. The teacher resolves to do her best to make up for this deficit in the child's life by giving him a maximum of attention. But the harder she tries, the less successful she is, and this makes her try even harder. The situation eventually turns into an impasse in which not only is the scholastic performance of this pupil falling well below the minimum, but the teacher is beginning to question her own worth.

She suspects that her nervousness may have something to do with the problem, and in typical common-sense fashion she tries to "pull herself together."

From her description it becomes quite obvious to the therapist that her solution, i.e., an inordinate amount of attention and help for this child, has created a problem out of an initial difficulty, and now perpetuates it. The teacher, of course, cannot immediately see this; common sense and what her psychology courses have taught her indicate that the problem is the child's broken home, his general unhappiness, etc., and what she tries is, in her view, the correct way of dealing with this problem.

It takes a good deal of reframing to make her willing to stop trying "more of the same," that is, not to single out this boy with her attention, but to deal with him in more or less the same way she deals with the rest of the class. Almost immediately the boy begins to seek *her* attention, first by means of some minor nuisances (which she is instructed to ignore) and soon by improved scholastic performance (which she is instructed to reward by immediate recognition and praise).

At the risk of being repetitious, we wish to point out that here, again, we asked ourselves *what* was going on here and now, not *why* the child was behaving the way he did, *why* the teacher felt the way she felt and then did what she did, etc.

We have found the same principle useful in dealing with runaway teenagers. In most of these cases the parents are understandably worried about the disappearance of their child, but also reluctant to call in the authorities and to make a missing persons report—especially if this is not the first time and if the previous escapades were relatively harmless capers. However, short of officially reporting the child's disappearance, the parents tend to leave no stone unturned to discover his whereabouts. If the parents can be persuaded to do absolutely nothing to trace him, not even to ask his friends, not to try to reach him through intermediaries, etc., the chances that the runaway will contact them quite soon are usually excellent. Of course, it may be asked how we can know that this would not have happened just as soon or sooner if the parents had instituted a search. All we can say is that from our interviews with these teenagers we have reason to believe that they are paying great attention to how much attention is being paid to their disappearance and that, consequently, the lack of noticeable attention (usually conveyed through the grapevine to the runaway by his peers) is a powerful reason to re-establish contact with their parents, while the knowledge of being the subject of an anxious search makes them likely to prolong the situation, which, after all, is but one variation of their typical relationship "game" with their parents.

Deliberate inattention in order to gain attention is the core element of a short story by the Viennese humorist Roda Roda. The young officers of an Austrian cavalry regiment, stationed in a desolate little town in Galicia, have just one ray of hope in their monotonous military routine: the cashier in the only café in town, a very charming, most desirable young lady. There she sits behind the counter, beleaguered by a crowd of eager, dashing officers, holding court and coyly rejecting all their advances. The hero of the story is desperately in love with her but knows that he has hardly a chance in competing with his fellow officers on their terms. He therefore adopts a deliberate strategy of inattention: he sits alone at his table, his back turned to her, and when he leaves the café he pays his bill to her with studied indifference. This makes him the only officer who is not after her and, human nature being what it is, enormously arouses her interest. Finally *she* goes after *him*, and, to the amazement of his comrades, who have tried every means of seduction known to them and have seen him do absolutely "nothing," he carries off the prize.

In the old days, a similar although converse use of attention and inattention was part of the match-making routine in Eastern European family tradition. Marriages were arranged by the parents and, quite understandably, their choice rarely met with great enthusiasm on the part of the two prospective spouses. In these cases the parents would usually avail themselves of the services of a professional match-maker who generally proceeded in the following way: He would first take one of the two, say the young man, aside and ask him if he had noticed how closely the girl was watching him whenever he did not look at her. Since the answer was likely to be negative, he was told to watch carefully but, of course, unobtrusively and he would see for himself. The prospective bride was then similarly instructed, and soon the two young people were quite interested in one another.

Study Problems

The efforts made by students to cope with their academic requirements are often of a typically counterproductive nature, and a recent example may stand, *mutatis mutandis,* for a whole group of similar problems.

An intelligent young man, studying for his master's degree, had particular difficulties when it came to writing papers and meeting the deadline for their presentation. Dreading this task, he would habitually postpone it until the last weekend, get up early on Saturday, and then sit at his desk, staring at a plentiful supply of paper and six sharpened pencils, but unable to write down even the first sentence. With the exception of a few hours of fitful sleep on Sunday morning, this agony would go on and increase until late Sunday night, when, in sheer desperation, he would concoct some sort of brief essay, partly by copying out of textbooks, and submit it on Monday morning to meet the deadline. Every time he did this he was convinced that he would receive a failing grade, but usually, always to his surprise, the paper would pass. In typical fashion he would then attribute this to some weird mistake or to the fact that the professor probably liked him enough to close both eyes to his deplorable production. Eventually the only requirements left for obtaining his degree were two papers. Being a typical example of the traveler who finds that "it is better to travel hopefully than to arrive," he went into a particularly agonizing orgy of procrastination. When he told us about this latest problem, he had already obtained two extensions of the deadline and there was no hope that he would be granted a third one. From earlier contacts with him we knew that he was imposing utopian demands on the quality of his work and was then forced into procrastination as the only avoidance tactic open to him. It was especially difficult for him to start writing, because no matter how he formulated the opening sentence, it simply was not good enough, and this prevented him from even thinking about the second sentence. The obvious suggestion was for him to write those two papers in a way that would just barely earn him passing grades, but this suggestion he flatly rejected. The idea of producing something mediocre on purpose was unacceptable to him, although he had to agree that the final result of his intense labor was usually quite mediocre anyway. But—and this was the crucial difference for him—bad as it might be, it was, after all, the outcome of an excruciating amount of honest, hard work. Yet, here it was Friday afternoon and he knew only too well that by Monday morning these two papers would not be ready if he followed his usual procedure. He was eventually willing to enter into a compromise: he would write one paper in his way, and as far as the other went, he would make every conceivable effort to write it badly enough to get only a C-minus passing grade. In particular, he committed himself to not changing the first version of the first sentence under any circumstances, and to creating some deliberate shortcomings if, on rereading the paper, it should seem too good for a C-minus grade.

The reader may guess the rest of the story. In his next session he reported that he had first written "our" paper in less than two hours, whereupon he settled down to composing "his," which took him practically all weekend. When he got the papers back, he had a C-minus on "his" and a B-plus on "ours." He was visibly shaken and wondered what kind of a world it was in which something like this could happen. As can be seen, in this case the reframing was done mostly by the circumstances of the situation itself; the inexorable passage of time simply forced him to abandon his premise, and we utilized this state of emergency, in addition to respecting his need to do things the hard way. It would, of course, have been less painful to him had we been able to reframe the problem in a way that would have been more congenial and therefore less threatening to his value system and outlook on life. But even so, this one experience did, in Wittgenstein's words, teach him a different game instead of his own, and he could no longer naïvely go on playing. A lasting change was thus accomplished in this session, and by dealing with the "tip of the iceberg" only, that is, without the benefit of any insight whatsoever into the reasons and the origin of his perfectionism.

Another way of dealing with this problem of procrastination and excruciating but futile efforts at concentration in studying is by setting a *time limit.* For example, the student is asked by what time he could reasonably be expected to finish a given assignment —say, nine o'clock in the evening. He is then made to promise that if he does not complete the assignment by nine he will be free to do whatever he wants to do that evening, *except* to continue studying. This prescription reframes leisure time as punishment, and with students who tend to think in terms of reward and punishment, usually no further explanation needs to be given. They are best told that the proof of the pudding lies in the eating.

Yet another useful technique is the *linking* of two problems, whereby one is prescribed as "punishment" for the other. For instance, if a student has trouble with both studying and dating, change can be effected in both areas by prescribing that if he fails to meet a specific study requirement, he will agree to ask a girl for a date the next day. Linking problems in this way is also the method of choice in many other human impasses.

Dealing with Utopias

Common sense suggests that the best way of dealing with problems arising from exaggerated goals is by pointing to their practical flaws and absurdities in the hope that the utopian will then see them. As is almost the rule in human problems, common-sense solutions are the most self-defeating and sometimes even the most destructive ones. To try to inject "reality" into utopias establishes and maintains a first-order change impasse through the introduction of the reciprocal member (i.e., common sense versus utopianism). The outcome is again group invariance, for, to paraphrase Lao-tzu, we can see common sense as common sense only because there are utopias.

This interdependence of common sense and extreme ideas becomes especially evident when dealing with ideas of psychotic proportions. The morbidly suspicious paranoiac is far from pacified by any attempt to point out to him that he has nothing to fear—"If they were not out to hurt me, they would not try so hard to reassure me" is his typical reaction, and again more of the one leads to more of the other.

Similarly, a person with very high-flying goals in life will not take kindly to any attempt to convince him to scale down his plans and to make them more realistic. For him this is nothing but an invitation to resign himself to a miserable, depressing way of living; therefore the language of common sense is the least appropriate or successful in dealing with him. What he does understand, only too well, is the language of utopia. Of course, common sense balks at the idea of feeding into, rather than opposing, that which needs to be changed. But we have already seen that the way to deal with a pessimist is to outdo his pessimism, and, analogously, the utopian will usually relinquish his utopias most quickly if they are taken beyond his own limits. The following excerpts from an interview with a twenty-nine-year-old student are intended to show this form of intervention. (Needless to say, what follows is not a complete case report, nor is this intervention in itself a "cure" for schizophrenia.)

The patient reported that he had just been released from a state hospital. He had been taken there three weeks earlier in an acutely psychotic state: "I just had so many hallucinations—they just got out of hand. The car turned into a space ship and the scenery changed into something like a hundred years from now and everything looked like the aftermath of a—everything looked like the artificial reconstruction of the world."

Upon being asked what he now wanted to do with himself, he sketched out a rather grandiose plan. He not only wanted to go to Los Angeles and study sitar playing under Ravi Shankar, but he expected this music to become the medium through which he would influence the Western world. At the same time he also wanted to study agriculture in order to utilize Chinese agricultural methods to feed the starving masses of the world. When the therapist agreed with these goals in principle but found them not sufficiently big, the patient countered this by beginning to talk about a far less ambitious plan, namely to get involved in a halfway house. During the last two years, he said, he had been too introverted, and he needed some social feedback to get out of the deep well of his inner world. The therapist again found this idea rather small: "If we can do anything at all here in ten meetings, it's the very minor thing of at least trying to clarify what would be worth doing and accomplishing both in terms of being worthwhile to the world and indicating that you had accomplished something worthwhile—to get a picture of what would be the direction."

In his reply the patient still maintained his grandiose outlook, but he began to talk more realistically about what he could do right now:

Sort of like the only direction I could envision, you know—there are like big huge masses of mankind—I can't figure out in my mind the Oriental —the two Oriental traditions of Mao and—and the one that I see ultimately in man, and the ultimate Hindu thing now is Ravi Shankar's music, because it's the most ethereal manifestation just outside true meditation. And then, when Mao Tse-tung is dealing with agriculture, you know, and agrarian reform, and the two—in my mind I just see the two as big blocks and the thing about a halfway house is the only thing I can think. I cannot go any further than that right now—either as a musician down in Los Angeles or the halfway house somewhere in Santa Cruz.

A few minutes later the same pattern occurred once again, and this time the patient finished up describing his difficulties in very plain language:

THERAPIST: This is how far you have been able to go in your thinking. So far your thinking on the matter of the halfway house or the school of music is rather concrete and practical. This is all right in its place, but to keep your mind that much on the practical is certain to constrain you in using your imagination to get to a higher level and to think in larger and more comprehensive terms.

PATIENT: Every time I go to a higher level, it is more abstract. It takes time and I don't have any—I'm out of, you know—these big, practical problems I am haunted by, you know, like I have to—I have run out of money and I have to get something immediately—that's the problem.

By consistently using this technique the therapist was able to bring the dialogue down to more and more practical levels.[3]

The "Devil's Pact"

For many people, their problem is a simple one—they delay taking a necessary action involving some risk and inconvenience.

---

[3]For technical reasons this patient could be seen for only three sessions. In the follow-up interview four months later he stated that instead of having started his music career, he had registered at a state college and was working towards his master's degree in philosophy. He commented that this provided him with a more rational, concrete basis as compared to music. He still had hallucinations but now just ignored them; they were "meaningless and banal."

The unemployed engineer who has become anxious over going for job interviews, or the young man who is too shy to approach women, come to mind as examples.

Their problem is compounded when they seek to attain their goal in non-risky ways, and their attitude then becomes overcautious. Friends and associates unwittingly escalate the problem by urging them to "take the step." They typically do this in a reassuring way, pointing out that there is little to fear: "There's nothing to it," etc. These well-meant encouragements are usually interpreted by the troubled friend as a gross underestimation of his ineptitude or of the actual risk of failure and rejection involved. If anything, the message, "You'll see, you can do it" increases his fear of failing.

When such a person enters therapy, he is fully entrenched in a dilemma: what he wishes to attain has become all the more important and urgent, since time, money, etc., are running out, and because of this urgency it is all the more imperative that no risk of failure be involved in the eventual action. If the therapist allows himself to be caught up in this dilemma, he will make suggestions as to how the patient can overcome his trepidation and take the necessary steps. The patient, after listening carefully and agreeably to these suggestions, will then rather adeptly discount them as being unfeasible, or predict that no opportunity will arise to carry them out, or say that he has tried them before with no avail—so why repeat something that is sure to fail? With each refusal, however, he typically returns to a direct or indirect request that the therapist come up with new suggestions, and the cycle is then repeated. Such therapy often terminates when the patient, having exhausted the therapist's wits, announces that treatment is getting nowhere and that some other therapist or therapy might now be more appropriate. (It is common for such patients to have been in several short-lived courses of treatment of different sorts.)

The "Devil's Pact" is a maneuver which allows the therapist to deal with the dilemma by side-stepping it altogether and, paradoxically, by meeting the business of risk head-on. Since the patient cannot deny his cautiousness, nor that there has been no change in his problem from earlier or current therapy, he is told that there is a plan which will make the attainment of his goal highly likely, but that since he will surely turn it down if it is merely presented as another suggestion, this plan will be disclosed to him only if he first promises to carry it out regardless of how difficult, inconvenient, or unreasonable it might seem. Without being given any details, he is told that the execution of the plan is well within his capability and that it will not be harmful or expensive. To further motivate the patient to agree, he is told: "If you have all the answers to your problem, you really don't need me, but if you don't have the answers, you need my help, and I feel I can give it only in this way." At this point the client is bound to try to get some hint as to what risks might be involved in the plan before agreeing to it, but the therapist maintains his original position of "no details prior to your commitment." Since the patient is already feeling some urgency of time, this can be utilized by telling him: "I realize I am asking a great deal of you— to give me a blank check, as it were. I think it would be appropriate to think this over carefully before deciding and then to let me know your answer next week." (By implication, a negative answer has already been defined as resulting in the termination of treatment.)

This maneuver puts the patient in a curious position: he can only respond yes or no. If he says no, without knowing what it is that he is rejecting, except that it would probably solve his problem, he is forced into making a decision. In addition, he is forced into having to acknowledge, if only by the implication of his negative choice, that his complaint is not all that important or urgent, in which case further therapy or shopping around for suggestions from friends becomes irrelevant. If he agrees, he is committed to follow an order from another person without the opportunity to censor it first through "reason" and "logic." Thus, in accepting or rejecting this "pact with the devil" he is taking at least as great a risk as that involved in doing something about his problem, since he has put himself blindly into the hands of another person. Once he has consented to this, it makes little difference whether the plan involves a safer, incremental approach to the risky situation or some more drastic or very different action, since the very act of agreeing to do whatever he may be asked to do is already a change from his original approach of "carefulness at all costs."

The "Devil's Pact" is a particularly clear example by means of which our theory of change can be summarized once more: As long as client and therapist both stay within the frame set by the former, the problem is bound to persist. Many different solutions can be attempted *within* this frame, but they invariably lead to the same outcome, namely zero second-order change. Within the frame, the question, "What else could the patient do?" leads only to more of the same problem which it is supposed to solve and establishes a Game Without End. The "Devil's Pact," on the other hand, deals with the *frame*, that is, with the class and not with its members. It replaces the old game with a new one in which a risk must be taken—even if it is only the risk of refusing the Pact.

11
THE WIDER HORIZON

THROUGHOUT this book we have tried to show that our approach to problem formation and resolution is by no means limited to clinical cases, but has much wider applicability in most areas of human interaction. If many of our examples are taken from the field of psychotherapy, this is merely because it is the area with which we are most familiar.

As we have tried to show, these basic principles are few, simple, and general; there is no reason why they cannot be applied to problems regardless of the size of the social system involved. Of course, larger systems are likely to be more complex and more difficult to explore and influence in practice, since they may involve more significant parties, sub-systems, and so on. On the other hand, it should not be assumed beforehand that our approach will be impossibly difficult to apply to large systems just because they have posed great difficulties to other approaches— especially if these approaches were of the same problem-engendering nature as the ones we have studied in the preceding chapters. The only reliable basis for judging the value of a method remains the result achieved by its application.

Looking at larger social systems, we find as common problems impasses, escalations, and grand programs that are structurally identical to those encountered in the more personal areas of human life:

1. All too often, differences in status, position, and interest among the members of a social system result not in constructive complementarity and effective cooperation but in persistent and obstructive stalemates—impasses with which all concerned are

unhappy, but which they are unable to change.

2. Where the different parties involved view themselves as separate and symmetrical, the outcome is often a more or less rapid escalation of conflict; these escalations are similar whether they involve two individuals, two countries, or two races.

3. As we have already mentioned in our discussion of the effects of utopias, very typical problems may arise as the result of programs that are intended to reach some highly desirable goal, but that "somehow" do not work out as envisioned—and, in fact, may lead in contrary directions.

This third type is of growing importance. While such failure may have little or no social repercussions where the life plan of an individual is concerned, it can cause enormous waste and frustration in the case of large government programs. It is our contention that, especially in this area, change can be implemented effectively by focusing on minimal, concrete goals, going slowly, and proceeding step by step, rather than strongly promoting vast and vague targets with whose desirability nobody would take issue, but whose attainability is a different question altogether.

For instance, the handling of many fundamental social problems—e.g., poverty, aging, crime—is customarily approached by separating these difficulties as entities unto themselves, as almost diagnostic categories, referring to essentially quite disparate problems and requiring very different solutions. The next step then is to create enormous physical and administrative structures and whole industries of expertise, producing increased incompetence in ever vaster numbers of individuals (89). We see this as a basically counterproductive approach to such social needs, an approach that requires a massive deviant population to support the raison d'être of these monolithic agencies and departments.

Yet another example is provided by the large problems surrounding addiction (to drugs, alcohol, and tobacco) which presently tend to be defined predominantly in physiological terms.

Correspondingly, the "corrective" measures are based on medication. But as the controversy over methadone treatments shows, the effect of these "medications" may come very close to that of the addictive substances which they are supposed to replace. On the basis of some direct experience in this area as well as our general principles, it appears highly likely that these heroic measures have a totally unintended but very powerful effect in building beliefs in the magical properties of these addictive substances and the near impossibility of solving the problems of addiction by any lesser means. No doubt the problems of addiction are serious, but they can be handled much better by viewing them as behavior problems essentially similar to many other such problems, and by paying primary attention to what kinds of wrong solutions are helping to maintain them.

To sum up: We see our basic views on problem formation and problem resolution, persistence and change, as usefully and appropriately applicable to human problems generally. We recognize, of course, that there are many kinds of conditions and events bearing on persistence and change that are themselves outside the sphere of human intervention: physical and chemical processes in the natural world, ranging from evolution to earthquakes; biological illnesses; certain accidents; and many others. Our views do not directly apply to these phenomena which we all must accept as givens—but they do apply to the way people attempt to deal with these "natural" circumstances, in the same way as they apply to people's handling of given social circumstances. And the world of human behavior clearly stands out today as that area in which our understanding and skills most need revision.

REFERENCES

1. Adler, Alfred. *The Practice and Theory of Individual Psychology.* New York: Harcourt, Brace, 1927, p. 235.
2. *Ibid. p. 246.*
3. *Agoraphobia: An Informative Guide to Overcoming Phobias.* Distributed by Terrap, 560 Oxford Avenue, Palo Alto, Calif. 94306.
4. Aichhorn, August. *Wayward Youth.* New York: Viking Press, 1936.
5. Ardrey, Robert. *The Social Contract: A Personal Enquiry into the Evolutionary Sources of Order and Disorder.* New York: Atheneum, 1970, p. 3.
6. *Ibid.,* p. 157.
7. *Ibid.,* p. 196.
8. *Ibid.,* pp. 286–87.
9. Aristotle. *Physica,* Book V/2 (225^b 14–16), translated by R. P. Hardie and R. K. Gaye. Oxford: Clarendon Press, 1930.
10. Ashby, W. Ross. *Design for a Brain.* New York: John Wiley, 1954.
11. Ashby, W. Ross. *An Introduction to Cybernetics.* London: Chapman & Hall, 1956.
12. *Ibid.,* p. 11.
13. *Ibid.,* p. 43.
14. *Ibid.,* p. 243.
15. Barten, Harvey H., ed. *Brief Therapies.* New York: Behavioral Publications, 1971.
16. Bateson, Gregory; Jackson, Don D.; Haley, Jay; and Weakland, John. "Toward a Theory of Schizophrenia." *Behavioral Science,* 1: 251–64, 1956.

17. Bateson, Gregory, and Jackson, Don D., "Some Varieties of Pathogenic Organization." In *Disorders of Communication*, ed. David McK. Rioch, Vol. 42, Research Publications. Association for Research in Nervous and Mental Disease, 1964, pp. 270–83.
18. Bateson, Gregory. *Steps to an Ecology of Mind.* New York: Ballantine Books, 1972, p. 279.
19. *Ibid.*, p. 282 n.
20. *Ibid.*, p. 283.
21. Bateson, Gregory. Personal communication.
22. Bell, Eric T. *Men of Mathematics.* New York: Simon and Schuster, 1937, p. 375.
23. Berne, Eric. *Games People Play.* New York: Grove Press, 1964, pp. 116–22.
24. Böhler, Eugen. "Voraussetzungen einer Ueberwindung der Währungskrise." *Neue Zürcher Zeitung*, No. 519 (November 7, 1971), p. 18.
25. Boltwood, Charles E.; Cooper, Michael R.; Fein, Victoria E.; and Washburn, Paul V. "Skyjacking, Airline Security, and Passenger Reaction: Toward a Complex Model for Prediction." *American Psychologist* 27: 539–45, 1972, p. 544.
26. Brinton, Crane. *The Lives of Talleyrand.* New York: W. W. Norton, 1936, pp. 190–91.
27. Bronowski, J. "The Logic of the Mind." *American Scientist*, 54: 1–14, 1966, p. 6.
28. Dostoyevsky, Fyodor M. *The Possessed.* New York: Modern Library, 1936, p. 409.
29. Erickson, Milton H. Personal communication.
30. Esterson, Aaron. *The Leaves of Spring.* Harmondsworth, England: Penguin Books, 1972.
31. Eulau, Heinz. "Reason and Relevance: Reflections on a Madness of our Time." *Student Lawyer*, 1: 16, 1972.
32. Ferreira, Antonio J. "Family Myth and Homeostasis." *Ar-*

chives of General Psychiatry, 9: 457–63, 1963, p. 458.
33. Ferreira, Antonio J. "Psychosis and Family Myth." Unpublished manuscript.
34. Frankl, Victor E. *The Doctor and the Soul.* New York: Alfred A. Knopf, 1957.
35. Frankl, Victor E. "Paradoxical Intention." *American Journal of Psychotherapy,* 14: 520–35, 1960.
36. Frankl, Victor E. *Man's Search for Meaning: An Introduction to Logotherapy.* New York: Pocket Books, 1963.
37. Frege, Gottlob. *Grundgesetze der Arithmetik, begriffsschriftlich abgeleitet* [Basic Laws of Arithmetic], Vol. 1. Jena: Verlag Hermann Pohle, 1893, p. 4.
38. Fry, William F., Jr. *Sweet Madness: A Study of Humor.* Palo Alto: Pacific Books, 1963.
39. Giraudoux, Jean. *The Apollo of Bellac.* In *Jean Giraudoux, Four Plays.* Adapted and with an introduction by Maurice Valency. Vol. 1. New York: Hill and Wang, 1958, p. 90.
40. *Ibid.,* p. 93.
41. Gödel, Kurt. "Ueber formal unentscheidbare Sätze der Principia Mathematica und verwandter Systeme I." *Monatshefte für Mathematik und Physik,* 38: 173–98, 1931. [English translation: "On Formally Undecidable Propositions of Principia Mathematica and Related Systems I." Edinburgh and London: Oliver & Boyd, 1962.]
42. Goffman, Erving. *Asylums: Essays on the Social Situations of Mental Patients and Other Inmates.* Garden City: Anchor Books, 1961.
43. Haley, Jay, ed. *Advanced Techniques of Hypnosis and Therapy: Selected Papers of Milton H. Erickson.* New York: Grune and Stratton, 1967.
44. *Ibid.,* p. 131.
45. Hilsman, Robert. *To Move a Nation.* Garden City: Doubleday, 1967, p. 223.
46. Howard, Nigel. "The Theory of Metagames." *General Sys-*

tems, 11: 167–86, 1966. (Yearbook of the Society for General Systems Research.)

47. Howard, Nigel. *Paradoxes of Rationality: Theory of Metagames and Political Behavior*. Cambridge: M.I.T. Press, 1971, p. xx.
48. *Ibid.*, p. 64.
49. Jackson, Don D. "The Question of Family Homeostasis." *Psychiatric Quarterly Supplement*, 31: 79–90, part 1, 1957.
50. Jackson, Don D. "Family Interaction, Family Homeostasis, and Some Implications for Conjoint Family Psychotherapy." In *Individual and Familial Dynamics*, ed. Jules Masserman. New York: Grune and Stratton, 1959, pp. 122–41.
51. Jackson, Don D. "Family Rules: The Marital Quid Pro Quo." *Archives of General Psychiatry*, 12: 589–94, 1965.
52. Jackson, Don D., and Haley, Jay. "Transference Revisited." *Journal of Nervous and Mental Disease*, 137: 363–71, 1963.
53. Jung, Carl G. *Symbols of Transformation*. New York: Bollingen Foundation, 1952, p. 375.
54. Kahn, Roy, chairman, panel on "The RAP Center: Seeing People Who Would Never Get Seen." Quoted from the preliminary program of the Forty-eighth Annual Meeting of the American Ortho-Psychiatric Association, 1971, p. 52.
55. Keyser, Cassius J. *Mathematical Philosophy: A Study of Fate and Freedom*. New York: Dutton, 1922, p. 203.
56. *Khrushchev Remembers*. With an introduction, commentary, and notes by Edward Crankshaw. Translated and edited by Strobe Talbott. Boston, Little, Brown, 1970, pp. 194–95.
57. *Ibid.*, p. 498.
58. Koestler, Arthur. *Darkness at Noon*. New York: Modern Library, 1941.
59. Koestler, Arthur. *The Act of Creation*. New York: Macmillan, 1964, p. 35.
60. *Ibid.*, p. 59.

61. Koestler, Arthur. *The Invisible Writing.* New York: Macmillan, 1969, p. 435.
62. Kuhn, Thomas S. *The Structure of Scientific Revolutions.* 2nd ed., enlarged. Chicago: University of Chicago Press, 1970, p. 122.
63. Kursh, Charlotte Olmsted. "The Benefits of Poor Communication." *Psychoanalytic Review,* 58: 198–208, 1971.
64. Laing, Ronald D. *Self and Others.* New York: Pantheon Books, 1969, pp. 108–24.
65. *Ibid.,* p. 124.
66. Laing, Ronald D. "Mystification, Confusion, and Conflict." In *Intensive Family Therapy: Theoretical and Practical Aspects,* ed. I. Boszormenyi-Nagy and J. L. Framo. New York: Harper & Row, 1965, pp. 343–63.
67. Laing, Ronald D.; Phillipson, H.; and Lee, A. Russell. *Interpersonal Perception.* New York: Springer, 1966, p. 8.
68. Laing, Ronald D. *Knots.* New York: Pantheon Books, 1970, pp. 1 and 55.
69. Lao Tsu. *Tao Te Ching.* Translated by Gia-Fu Feng and Jane English. New York: Vintage Books, 1972.
70. Lasègue, Ch., and Falret, J. "La folie à deux, ou folie communiquée." Annales Médico-Psychologiques, t. 18, novembre 1877. [English translation by Richard Michaud, *American Journal of Psychiatry,* supplement to Vol. 121, No. 4, pp. 2–18, 1964.]
71. Lennard, Henry L., *et al. Mystification and Drug Abuse.* San Francisco: Jossey-Bass, 1971.
72. Leonhard, Wolfgang. *Child of the Revolution.* Translated by C. M. Woodhouse. Chicago: Henry Regnery, 1958, esp. pp. 197–208.
73. Lidz, Theodore; Cornelison, Alice; Terry, Dorothy; and Fleck, Stephen. "Intrafamilial Environment of the Schizophrenic Patient: VI. The Transmission of Irrationality." *Archives of Neurology and Psychiatry,* 79: 305–16, 1958.

74. Lipson, Leon. *How to Argue in Soviet.* Unpublished lectures, Stanford University, April, 1969.
75. Masterman, J.C. *The Double-Cross System in the War of 1939 to 1945.* New Haven: Yale University Press, 1972, p. 43.
76. Orwell, George. *1984.* New York: Harcourt, Brace, 1949.
77. Osgood, Charles E. "Reciprocal Initiative." In *The Liberal Papers,* ed. James Roosevelt. Chicago: Quadrangle Books, 1962, p. 172.
78. Popper, Karl R. "Utopia and Violence." In *Conjectures and Refutations.* New York: Basic Books, 1962, chap. 18, p. 361.
79. Premack, Ann James, and Premack, David. "Teaching Language to an Ape." *Scientific American,* 227: 92–9, October, 1972.
80. Prior, Arthur N. *Changes in Events and Changes in Things.* The Lindley Lecture, Department of Philosophy, University of Kansas, 1962, p. 3.
81. Rosenthal, Robert. *Experimenter Effects in Behavioral Research.* New York: Appleton-Century-Crofts, 1966.
82. Salzman, L. "Reply to Critics." *International Journal of Psychiatry,* 6: 473–6, 1968.
83. Scheflen, Albert E. "Regressive One-to-One Relationships." *Psychiatric Quarterly,* 23: 692–709, 1960.
84. Schopenhauer, Arthur. *Über den Willen in der Natur.* In *Arthur Schopenhauers sämtliche Werke,* Vol. III. Munich: R. Piper, 1912, p. 346 (our translation).
85. Sluzki, Carlos E., and Verón, Eliseo. "The Double Bind as a Universal Pathogenic Situation." *Family Process,* 10: 397–410, 1971.
86. Symposium on Training. *Journal of Analytical Psychology,* 6: 95–118, 1961.
87. Szasz, Thomas S. "Psycho-analytic Training." *International Journal of Psycho-Analysis,* 39: 589–613, 1958.

88. Tarski, Alfred. *Logic, Semantics, Metamathematics: Papers from 1923 to 1938.* Translated by J. H. Woodger. Oxford: Clarendon Press, 1956.
89. Thayer, Lee. "The Functions of Incompetence." In *Festschrift for Henry Margenau,* ed. E. Laszlo and Emily B. Sellow. New York: Gordon & Breach, in preparation.
90. Thomas, William Isaac as quoted by Sylvia Sussman in "An Approach to the Study of Family Interaction: What a Family Is." *Views Magazine,* Summer, 1965.
91. Watzlawick, Paul. *An Anthology of Human Communication; Text and Tape.* Palo Alto: Science & Behavior Books, 1964, p. 21.
92. Watzlawick, Paul; Beavin, Janet H.; and Jackson, Don D. *Pragmatics of Human Communication: A Study of Interactional Patterns, Pathologies and Paradoxes.* New York: W. W. Norton, 1967, pp. 51–54 and 80–93.
93. *Ibid.,* pp. 54–59 and 93–99.
94. *Ibid.,* pp. 187–256.
95. *Ibid.,* pp. 230–31.
96. *Ibid.,* pp. 230–53.
97. *Ibid.,* pp. 232–36.
98. *Ibid.,* p. 235.
99. Weakland, John H. and Jackson, Don D. "Patient and Therapist Observations on the Circumstances of a Schizophrenic Episode." *Archives of Neurology and Psychiatry,* 79: 554–74, 1958.
100. Weissberg, A. *The Accused.* New York: Simon and Schuster, 1951.
101. Whitehead, Alfred North, and Russell, Bertrand. *Principia Mathematica.* 2nd ed. 3 vol. Cambridge: Cambridge University Press, 1910–13, Vol. 1, p. 37.
102. Wittgenstein, Ludwig. *Tractatus Logico-Philosophicus.* New York: Humanities Press, 1951, p. 187.
103. *Ibid.,* p. 189.
104. Wittgenstein, Ludwig. *Remarks on the Foundations of*

Mathematics. Oxford: Basil Blackwell, 1956, p. 100.

105. *Ibid,* pp. 179 and 181.
106. Wittgenstein, Ludwig. *Philosophical Investigations.* 2nd ed. Translated by G. E. M. Anscomb. New York: Macmillan, 1958, p. 3.
107. *Ibid.,* p. 19.
108. *Ibid.,* p. 103.
109. *Ibid.,* p. 134.
110. Wynne, Lyman C.; Ryckoff, Irving M.; Day, Juliana; and Hirsch, Stanley I. "Pseudo-Mutuality in the Family Relations of Schizophrenics." *Psychiatry,* 21: 205–20, 1958.
111. Yalom, Irvin, and Yalom, Marilyn, "Ernest Hemingway: The Psychiatric View." *Archives of General Psychiatry,* 24: 485–94, 1971.

AUTHOR AND SUBJECT INDEX

(Page numbers in bold type refer to definitions)

169